\

Quantifying Software Reliability at Early Development Stages

Wende Kong

Quantifying Software Reliability at Early Development Stages

A Formal and Scalable Approach

VDM Verlag Dr. Müller

Impressum/Imprint (nur für Deutschland/ only for Germany)

Bibliografische Information der Deutschen Nationalbibliothek: Die Deutsche Nationalbibliothek verzeichnet diese Publikation in der Deutschen Nationalbibliografie; detaillierte bibliografische Daten sind im Internet über http://dnb.d-nb.de abrufbar.
Alle in diesem Buch genannten Marken und Produktnamen unterliegen warenzeichen-, marken- oder patentrechtlichem Schutz bzw. sind Warenzeichen oder eingetragene Warenzeichen der jeweiligen Inhaber. Die Wiedergabe von Marken, Produktnamen, Gebrauchsnamen, Handelsnamen, Warenbezeichnungen u.s.w. in diesem Werk berechtigt auch ohne besondere Kennzeichnung nicht zu der Annahme, dass solche Namen im Sinne der Warenzeichen- und Markenschutzgesetzgebung als frei zu betrachten wären und daher von jedermann benutzt werden dürften.

Coverbild: www.purestockx.com

Verlag: VDM Verlag Dr. Müller Aktiengesellschaft & Co. KG
Dudweiler Landstr. 99, 66123 Saarbrücken, Deutschland
Telefon +49 681 9100-698, Telefax +49 681 9100-988, Email: info@vdm-verlag.de
Zugl.: College Park, University of Maryland, Diss., 2009

Herstellung in Deutschland:
Schaltungsdienst Lange o.H.G., Berlin
Books on Demand GmbH, Norderstedt
Reha GmbH, Saarbrücken
Amazon Distribution GmbH, Leipzig
ISBN: 978-3-639-19273-5

Imprint (only for USA, GB)

Bibliographic information published by the Deutsche Nationalbibliothek: The Deutsche Nationalbibliothek lists this publication in the Deutsche Nationalbibliografie; detailed bibliographic data are available in the Internet at http://dnb.d-nb.de .
Any brand names and product names mentioned in this book are subject to trademark, brand or patent protection and are trademarks or registered trademarks of their respective holders. The use of brand names, product names, common names, trade names, product descriptions etc. even without a particular marking in this works is in no way to be construed to mean that such names may be regarded as unrestricted in respect of trademark and brand protection legislation and could thus be used by anyone.

Cover image: www.purestockx.com

Publisher:
VDM Verlag Dr. Müller Aktiengesellschaft & Co. KG
Dudweiler Landstr. 99, 66123 Saarbrücken, Germany
Phone +49 681 9100-698, Fax +49 681 9100-988, Email: info@vdm-publishing.com

Printed in the U.S.A.
Printed in the U.K. by (see last page)
ISBN: 978-3-639-19273-5

Preface

Problems which originate in early development stages can have a lasting influence on the reliability, safety, and cost of a software system. The requirements document, which is usually available at the requirements analysis stage, must be correct, unambiguous, and complete if the rest of the development effort is to succeed. The ability to identify faults in requirements and predict the reliability of a software system early in its development can help organizations make informative decisions about corrective actions and improve the system's quality in a cost-effective manner. A review of the literature reveals that existing approaches are unsuited to provide trustworthy reliability prediction either due to the ignorance of the requirements documents, or because of the informal and fairly sketchy way in detecting faults in requirements.

This book is a direct outgrowth of the author's doctoral study at University of Maryland, Collect Park, USA. The study explores the use of a preselected software reliability measurement for early software faults detection and reliability prediction. This measurement, originally a black-box testing technique, was broadly recognized for its ability to detect incomplete and ambiguous requirements, although no information was found in the literature about how to take advantage of its power. The study mathematically formalized the measurement to enhance its rigidity, repeatability and scalability and further extended it as an effective requirements faults detection technique. An automation-oriented algorithm was developed for quantifying the impact of the detected requirements faults on software reliability. The feasibility

i

and scalability of the proposed approach for early faults detection and reliability prediction were examined using two real applications. The results clearly confirmed its feasibility and usefulness, particularly when no failure data is available and other methods are not applicable. The scalability barriers were also spotted in the approach. An empirical study was thus conducted to gain insight into the nature of the technical barriers. As an attempt to overcome the barrier, a set of rules was proposed based on the observed patterns. Finally, a preliminarily controlled experiment was conducted to evaluate the usability of the proposed rules.

The study will allow software project stakeholders to effectively detect requirements faults and assess the quality of requirements early in development, and ultimately lead to improved software reliability if the identified faults are removed in time. Software project practitioners, regulators, and policy makers involved in the certification of software systems can benefit most from the techniques proposed in the study.

Dedication

For my father, Mr. Qinglu Kong, and mother, Mrs. Qiu'e Chen, without whom nothing would be much worth doing;

And in memory of my loving grandmother, Mrs. Yazhen Ma, who died at her 99 years old when this book was written, and my uncle, Mr. Qingrong Knog, who always encouraged me to follow my dreams.

Table of Contents

Preface.. i

Dedication iii

List of Tables viii

List of Figures x

Chapter 1: Introduction.. 1

    1.1 Research Statement.. 1

    1.2 Research Objective 3

    1.3 Approach.. 4

    1.4 Content.. 5

    1.5 Summary of Contributions.. 7

Chapter 2: Background and Related Work 9

    2.1 Definitions 9

    2.2 Current Situation... 10

    2.3 Reliability Measurement vs. Development Phases.. 12

    2.4 Brief Taxonomy of Software Reliability Measurement Models 15

    2.5 Why Early Reliability Measurement is Necessary 18

        2.5.1 Majority of Software Projects Failed to Achieve Schedule and Budget Goal 18

        2.5.2 Requirements are the Root of Many Problems 19

        2.5.3 Faults Cost Less when Detected and Fixed in Early Stages of Development.. 21

    2.6 Virtues of Early Software Reliability Measurement... 26

    2.7 Previous Work on Early Reliability Measurement 27

    2.8 Selecting Software Measurement for Early Reliability Assessment 31

Chapter 3: Formalization of Cause-Effect Graphing Analysis as a Software Reliability Measurement... 35

    3.1 What is Cause-Effect Graphing Analysis (CEGA).. 35

    3.2 Construction of CEG 37

    3.3 CEGA as a Software Reliability Measurement 38

3.4 Advantages and Disadvantages of CEGA 41

3.5 Formal Definition of CEG 49

3.6 Example of CEG Construction 53

    3.6.1 Identified Causes, Effects, Logical Relationships, and Constraints for the
Sample SRS 55

    3.6.2 Graphical Expression of CEG for the Sample SRS 56

    3.6.3 Mathematical Expression of CEG for the Sample SRS 56

3.7 Summary 57

Chapter 4: Identification of Faults in Software Requirements Specifications Using
CEGA 58

4.1 Definition, Contents, and Organization of SRSs 59

4.2 Characteristics of a "Good" SRS 62

4.3 Faults in SRS 63

4.4 V&V Techniques for SRS Faults Detection 66

4.5 CEGA-based Techniques for SRS Faults Detection 68

    4.5.1 CEGA-based SRS Faults Taxonomy 69

    4.5.2 Detecting SRS Faults by CEG Construction and Optional Ambiguities
Review 70

    4.5.3 Detecting More Implicit SRS Faults by CEG Validation 72

4.6 Summary 76

    4.6.1 Advantages of our Methods 77

    4.6.2 Limitations of our Methods 77

Chapter 5: Quantification of the Impact of Faults on Software Reliability 79

5.1 Basic Notations and Definitions 79

5.2 Fundamental Lemma and Overall Algorithm for Quantifying Software
Reliability 82

5.3 Determination of Failure-relevant Inputs 85

    5.3.1 Introduction of B-CEG 85

    5.3.2 Rules for B-CEG Construction and A-CEG Revision 88

    5.3.3 Introduction of Virtual Effect for Mating Missing or Extra Effects 91

    5.3.4 Determination of an Effect's Output 93

5.3.5 Algorithm for Determining the Category of an Input............................ 95

5.3.6 Examples of Identifying Failure-relevant Inputs 97

5.4 Calculation of the Occurrence Probability of Failure-relevant Inputs........... 107

5.4.1 Representation of a Boolean Expression Using BDD Techniques...... 109

5.4.2 Recursive Algorithm for Calculating the Occurrence Probability of a BDD's Top Node... 111

5.4.3 Operational Profile (OP)... 113

5.5 Summary.. 114

Chapter 6: Examination of the Applicability of the Proposed CEGA Techniques for Early-stage Software Reliability Prediction by Case Studies 115

6.1 Applications Used Case Studies 116

6.2 Procedure 117

6.3 Results and Findings... 119

6.4 Summary... 127

Chapter 7: Exploration of the Scalability of A-CEG Construction 128

7.1 Objectives 129

7.2 Methodology and Procedure 130

7.2.1 Step 1: Experiment Preparation 130

7.2.2 Step 2: Implementation of the Independent Study Project 132

7.2.3 Step 3: Postmortem Analysis and Improvement................................ 136

7.3 Results and Discussion 138

7.3.1 The Database of Rules and Indicators for A-CEG Elements Identification.. 138

7.3.2 The A-CEG Construction Rules 139

7.3.3 Potential Influencing Factors of A-CEG Construction 153

7.3.4 Suggestions for Writing an SRS 156

7.4 Summary... 158

Chapter 8: Validation of the Usability of the A-CEG Construction Rules............... 160

8.1 Definitions 161

8.2 Research Questions and Hypotheses 169

8.3 Variables 171

8.3.1 Independent Variables 172

8.3.2 Controlled Variables 172

8.3.3 Dependent Variables 173

8.4 Subjects 173

8.5 Experiment Materials 174

8.6 Procedure 178

8.6.1 Training and Preparation (Phase I) 178

8.6.2 Running the Experiment (Phase II) 180

8.7 Experiment Results and Discussion 184

8.7.1 Statistical Analysis 184

8.7.2 Summary of Statistical Testing 198

8.7.3 Qualitative Analysis 199

8.8 Threats to Validity 201

8.9 Summary 202

Chapter 9: Conclusion and Suggestions for Future Research 204

9.1 Principal Results of this Study and its Significance 204

9.2 Advantages 208

9.3 Limitations 210

9.4 Suggestions for Future Research 211

Appendix A: List of Words that Point to Potential Ambiguities (adapted from [70]) 215

Appendix B: Sample Source Code for Calculating the Occurrence Probability of a BDD's Top Node 218

Appendix C: Results of Case Study A 222

Appendix D: Descriptions of the Database's Rules in Empirical Study C 228

Appendix E: Reporting Tables Used in Experiment D 230

Appendix F: The First Questionnaire Used in Experiment D 233

Appendix G: Postmortem Questionnaire Used in Experiment D (to assess usability of the A-CEG Construction Rules set) 235

Glossary 236

Bibliography 237

List of Tables

Table 2-1: Phase-based Applicability and Ranking Classification of 40 Software
Reliability Measurements 33

Table 3-1: Mathematical Symbols of CEG Constraints 51

Table 3-2: Identified Causes for the Sample SRS 55

Table 3-3: Identified Effects for the Sample SRS 55

Table 3-4: Identified Constraints for the Sample SRS.. 56

Table 4-1: Ten Language Quality Characteristics of an SRS (Adapted from [67]) ... 62

Table 4-2: Taxonomy of SRS Faults (Excerpted from [68]) 64

Table 4-3: Categories of SRS Faults in Terms of CEG 70

Table 5-1: Faults vs. Actions that should be taken for A-CEG or B-CEG 90

Table 5-2: Effects' Outputs for Case 1 99

Table 5-3: Effects' Outputs for Case 2 100

Table 5-4: Effects' Outputs for Case 3 101

Table 5-5: Effects' Outputs for Case 4 103

Table 5-6: Effects' Outputs for Case 5 104

Table 5-7: Effects' Outputs for Case 6 105

Table 5-8: Effects' Outputs for Case 7 107

Table 6-1: Steps vs. Required Techniques/Tools 118

Table 6-2: Scalability of the Proposed Techniques 120

Table 6-3: A-CEGs and CE(%) for PACS and SXXX 121

Table 6-4: Number of Detected Faults vs. Efforts in Using SRS-related Measurements
.... 123

Table 7-1: Example Items Used to Develop Rule 7-1 and Rule 7-11 136

Table 7-2: Mapping of the Database's Rules to the A-CEG Construction Rules..... 139

Table 8-1: Results of the Preliminary Study for Determining the Threshold Relative
Inter-textual Distance... 166

Table 8-2: Results of Testing the Population Mean of Either Style I's or Style's
Relative Inter-textual Distances against the Selected Threshold Value (α
= 0.05)... 168

Table 8-3: Basic Information on SRS Segments Used in Experiment D 176

Table 8-4: Data on SRS Segments Used in Experiment Phase II............................ 177

Table 8-5: Assignments of SRS Segments 182

Table 8-6: Entire Design of Experiment D 183

Table 8-7: Experiment Data Used for Hypotheses Testing 184

Table 8-8: Descriptive Statistics for the Impact of A-CEG Construction Method on
Effectiveness 186

Table 8-9: Statistical Testing Results for Hypothesis H1 ($\alpha = 0.05$) 187

Table 8-10: Descriptive statistics for the Impact of A-CEG Construction Method on
Efficiency 188

Table 8-11: Statistical Testing Results for Hypothesis H2 ($\alpha = 0.05$) 189

Table 8-12: Descriptive Statistics for the Impact of SRS' Writing Styles on
Effectiveness 190

Table 8-13: Statistical Testing Results for Hypothesis H3 ($\alpha = 0.05$) 191

Table 8-14: Descriptive Statistics for the Impact of SRS' Writing Style on Efficiency
.... 192

Table 8-15: Statistical Testing Results for Hypothesis H4 ($\alpha = 0.05$) 193

Table 8-16: Descriptive Statistics for the Impact of SRS' Application Type on
Effectiveness 194

Table 8-17: Statistical Testing Results for Hypothesis H5 ($\alpha = 0.05$) 195

Table 8-18: Descriptive Statistics for the Impact of SRS' Application Type on
Efficiency 196

Table 8-19: Statistical Testing Results for Hypothesis H6 ($\alpha = 0.05$) 197

Table 8-20: Summary of Statistical Tests 199

Table 8-21: Experiment data for Qualitative Analysis 199

Table Appendix C-1: Definitions of Effects' in PACS' A-CEG and B-CEG 226

Table Appendix C-2: PACS' OP 227

ix

List of Figures

Figure 2-1: Relationship among the Error, Fault, and Failure 10

Figure 2-2: Software Reliability Measurement vs. Development Process 15

Figure 2-3: Brief Taxonomy of Software Reliability Measurement Models 17

Figure 2-4: Outcomes of Department of Defense Software Spending 18

Figure 2-5: Distribution of Faults in Software Projects 20

Figure 2-6: Distribution of Failure Causes of 8000+ projects 21

Figure 2-7: Distribution of Effort to Fix Faults 22

Figure 2-8: Industry Standard Cost Ratio to Fix a Defect 22

Figure 2-9: Cost Ratio vs. Development Phases in Which Faults are Found 23

Figure 2-10: Summation Effect of Faults 25

Figure 2-11: Development Schedule with/without Early Fault Detection 27

Figure 3-1: Symbols of Basic CEG Logical Relationships 36

Figure 3-2: Symbols of CEG Constraints 36

Figure 3-3: Example of Identifying Causes and Effects in an SRS 54

Figure 3-4: Graphical Expression of CEG for the Sample SRS 56

Figure 3-5: Mathematical Expression of CEG for the Sample SRS 57

Figure 4-1: Prototype Outline of SRS (extracted from IEEE Std. 830-1998 [53]) 61

Figure 4-2: Desired vs. Actually Documented Requirements Specifications 63

Figure 4-3: Requirements Fault Categorization Percentage Data 66

Figure 4-4: CEG Validation Algorithm 73

Figure 5-1: CEGA-based Software Reliability Prediction Algorithm 85

Figure 5-2: Software Testing Using Test Oracle 86

Figure 5-3: Identifying Failure-relevant Inputs Using B-CEG 87

Figure 5-4: Example of Adding Virtual Effects into A-CEG and B-CEG 93

Figure 5-5: Unified Process for Determining the Output of an Effect 95

Figure 5-6: Algorithm for Determining the Category of a Given Input $\overline{x}^k$ 97

Figure 5-7: Mathematical Expression of the Sample A-CEG 98

Figure 5-8: Revised A-CEG and B-CEG for Case 1 98

Figure 5-9: Revised A-CEG and B-CEG for Case 2 100

Figure 5-10: Revised A-CEG and B-CEG for Case 3 101

Figure 5-11: Revised A-CEG and B-CEG for Case 4 102

Figure 5-12: Revised A-CEG and B-CEG for Case 5 103

Figure 5-13: Revised A-CEG and B-CEG for Case 6 105

Figure 5-14: Revised A-CEG and B-CEG for Case 7 106

Figure 5-15: Generic Fault Tree Model for A-CEG 108

Figure 5-16: Example of BDD for the Boolean Function $f = xy + z$ 110

Figure 5-17: Recursive Algorithm for Calculating the Occurrence Probability of a
BDD's Top Node 112

Figure 6-1: Distribution of Detected Faults in Case Study A (for PACS)................ 121

Figure 6-2: Distribution of Detected Faults in Case Study B (for SXXX)............... 122

Figure 6-3: Distribution of Logical Relationships in PACS' A-CEG 122

Figure 6-4: Distribution of Logical Relationships in SXXX's A-CEG 122

Figure 6-5: Number of Detected Faults vs. Effort for PACS 124

Figure 6-6: Number of Detected Faults vs. Effort for SXXX................................... 124

Figure 6-7: Distribution of Efforts in Case Study A (for PACS) 125

Figure 6-8: Distribution of Efforts in Case Study B (for SXXX)............................ 125

Figure 7-1: Timeline for Implementing the Independent Study Project.................. 132

Figure 7-2: Workflow for Extracting Rules and Indicators for identification of A-
CEG Elements 134

Figure 7-3: Process Used to Distill the A-CEG Construction Rules 137

Figure 7-4: Number of Rules Extracted from Selected SRSs................................... 138

Figure 7-5: Number of Indicators Extracted from Selected SRSs........................... 138

Figure 7-6: Suggested Workflow for Using the A-CEG Construction Rules........... 150

Figure 8-1: Confusion Matrix 162

Figure 8-2: Impact of A-CEG construction method on the Effectiveness................ 187

Figure 8-3: Impact of A-CEG Construction Method on Efficiency 189

Figure 8-4: Impact of Writing Style on Effectiveness 191

Figure 8-5: Impact of Writing Style on Efficiency 193

Figure 8-6: Impact of Application Type on Effectiveness.. 195

Figure 8-7: Impact of Application Type on Efficiency 197

Figure Appendix C-1: Graphical Expression of PACS's A-CEG 222

Figure Appendix C-2: Mathematical Expression of PACS's A-CEG 223

Figure Appendix C-3: Graphical Expression of PACS's B-CEG 224

Figure Appendix C-4: Mathematical Expression of PACS's B-CEG 225

Chapter 1: Introduction

1.1 Research Statement

Initiating software reliability prediction earlier in the software development lifecycle is critical in the success of implementing high quality software systems in today's fast-paced development environment, because early prediction of software reliability can help organizations make informed decisions about corrective actions in a cost-effective manner.

Early estimations and predictions of software quality attributes are essential for control of software development and delivery of software products. In fact, the literature reveals that the use of early-stage software reliability models may well contribute to project success, as it enables the early detection and addressing of risks and issues of concern in an early stage of the project. Especially, time spent early on making sure that requirements are correct and has been observed saving much time and effort later. It has been shown many times that a bug found in the early stages of the product lifecycle is cheaper, in terms of money, effort and time, to fix than the same bug found later on in the process. As programming and test techniques have improved, the bugs have shifted closer to the process front end, to requirements and their specifications. Because they are first-in and last-out, faults originating in requirements are the costliest of all. These faults, like wrong, incomplete, and inconsistent requirements, cause costly development cycles, delay time to market, and lower product quality. Inspection of a requirements document can detect faults in an

1

early stage of development, improve software quality, and prevents effort for unnecessary rework. However, existing methods for requirements faults detection are mostly informal and fairly sketchy. Therefore, any research aiming at a systematic derivation or even an automatic detection of requirements faults is of great practical importance.

Studies describe what has been the industry reality for decades: the majority of software projects fail to achieve schedule and budget goals. As a result, there is an ever-increasing need for an affordable early predictor for software projects in academia, industry, and government. The purpose of such a predictor is to identify projects that were likely to be at high risk of failure in a very early stage. This would enable the project stakeholders to take corrective actions before significant resources have been expended in accordance with problematic requirements. Most of the existing software reliability models are applicable only in the testing phase when failure data are available. This is too late for affordably guiding corrective action to improve the quality of the software. Although some approaches have been proposed for early reliability prediction, common problems prevent these approaches from being practicable. These problems are: lack of generic applicability and scalability, over-dependence on industry-average data, such as faults content per function point, and/or ignorance of product documents. In particular, Software Requirements Specifications documents (SRS), the most significant documents usually available at the end of requirements analysis phase, are neglected by these approaches due to difficulties in linking requirements-based measurement(s) to reliability. Therefore, they are inevitably inadequate to provide trustworthy results.

Apparently, a new approach is required to bridge the gap between requirements-based measurement(s) and reliability quantification. This probabilistic-reliability prediction approach should also enable software professionals to identify problematic requirements to reduce the risks of projects.

1.2 *Research Objective*

The objective of the study is to develop an approach that would allow the project stakeholders to determine at a very early development stage the problematic areas in the requirements and whether or not the project is at high risk of failure. The results of the study should be of value to the organization and project managers as they can assess the risks of a project at an earlier stage and either mitigate the risks before it is too late to do so or cancel the project. More specifically, this study is to investigate how to detect problematic requirements specifications and how software reliability assessment can be achieved at requirements analysis phase while limited information about the software project is available.

To achieve this, the following critical questions need to be answered:

- Are there quantifiable features that can be extracted from information available in early stages that can be used to help predict software reliability?
- What should be measured for software reliability prediction at early development stages? What is the right data to collect and what is the right way to process the collected data?
- What are the limitations of the approach? Is the approach feasible and scalable?

1.3 Approach

This study deals with software reliability prediction on the basis of assessing the quality of the plain-text requirements specifications, which are usually available at the end of the requirements analysis phase, a very early stage of development.

Our approach begins with selecting the right one out of 40 ranked software reliability measurements according to several predefined criteria, such as the applicability at early stages, repeatability, potential in usability and scalability, and so on. These measurements were ranked with respect to its ability at predicting software reliability through an expert opinion elicitation process and the ranking was partially validated in our previous research.

After thoroughly analyzing its advantages, disadvantages, and other technical barriers as a software reliability measurement, we mathematically formalize the selected measurement to enhance its rigidity, repeatability, and scalability. We further investigate its ability in detecting problematic requirements specifications and develop a systematic method for requirements faults detection on the basis of the enhanced measurement.

We develop a unique automation-oriented algorithm to quantify the impact of the detected requirements faults on software reliability. The quantification algorithm is based on the use of the formalized measurement, the Binary Decision Diagram techniques, and a recursive algorithm developed in this study. Moreover, this quantification algorithm uses detected faults instead of the number of faults because the former is believed to provide a more solid foundation for reliability quantification.

4

We also introduce artifacts and develop techniques to enable the automation of the quantification algorithm.

We then apply our approach to two real applications, one smaller and the other larger, to examine the feasibility and scalability of the proposed techniques for detecting SRS faults and predicting the reliability at requirement analysis phase. After the feasibility is clearly confirmed, we focus on identifying the scalability bottlenecks in our approach.

We employ the empirical study approach to gain insight into the nature of the technical barriers on scalability because quantitative research requires large sample sizes and such a sampling is not feasible for this study. We collect and distill the patterns observed in the empirical study, and develop rule-based methods to overcome these barriers. The influencing factors are identified and analyzed as well.

Finally, a controlled experiment is conducted to evaluate the usability of the proposed techniques/methods addressing the technical barriers. Due to the lack of enough resources to reliably test the effects of all identified influencing factors, we only statistically verify the impact of two influencing factors on using the proposed techniques/methods while the impact of other factors could be significant.

1.4 *Content*

The rest of this dissertation is organized as follows:

In Chapter 2 we discuss the background and researches related to this study, and provide readers with the details on how we selected a software reliability measurement for this study.

Chapter 3 focuses on exploring the advantages and disadvantages of the selected measurement. Several attempts to enhance the measurement towards a scalable software reliability prediction technique are discussed. Especially, the mathematical expression of the measurement is defined in terms of well understood mathematical entities, such as sets and Boolean formula, whose semantics are formally defined and can be easily stored and processed by computers. At the end of this chapter, we illustrate the use of the enhanced measurement with a simple example.

Chapter 4 introduces the concept of Software Requirements Specifications (SRS), attributes of a "good" SRS, commonly seen SRS faults, and existing techniques for SRS faults detection. The remainder of this chapter discusses our disciplined methods proposed for systematically detecting faults in natural language SRSs.

Chapter 5 describes the unique automation-oriented algorithm proposed for quantifying the impact of the detected SRS faults on software reliability. This algorithm is based on the formalized measurement and applicable in requirements analysis stage and other development stages.

Chapter 6 reports the procedure, results, and analysis of two case studies: Case Study A and Case Study B. These two case studies were conducted to evaluate the feasibility and scalability of the proposed CEGA techniques for quantification of software reliability at the requirements analysis stage.

Chapter 7 presents the objectives, procedure, detailed findings and analysis pertinent to Empirical Study C, which focuses on gaining insight into the nature of the scalability barriers identified in our approach. A set of rules attempting to overcome the scalability barrier is also proposed and presented in this chapter.

Chapter 8 provides the pertinent information about a small-scale controlled experiment, called Experiment D. This experiment aims at comparing and evaluating how well the rules set proposed in Chapter 7 performs in comparison to other methods, and investigating whether the rules set succeeds in its goals of providing the same or improved benefits, with what cost, and under what circumstances it makes the most sense. The hypotheses about the impact of two factors (the SRS' writing style and SRS' application type) on the effectiveness and efficiency of using the rules set are formulated and tested.

In Chapter 9, we discuss restrictions and limitations on the use of our approach, conclude the study, and propose some suggestions for future research.

1.5 Summary of Contributions

The significant contributions of this study are as follows:

1. Development of a method for systematical detection of faults in natural language requirements. This method is based on an existing technique originally used for black-box testing. This study thoroughly discusses this technique to compensate for the obvious absence of review papers in this area, mathematically formalizes this technique, and enhances its rigidity, repeatability, and scalability towards a scalable software reliability

7

measurement applicable to the analysis of natural language requirements. The enhanced technique is further extended to a new method capable of systematically detecting faults in requirements. This method allows software project stakeholders to identify the problematic areas in the requirements at a very early development stage. Moreover, this method overcomes the shortcomings of other techniques that fail to ensure complete coverage of functional requirements.

2. Development of a method for quantifying the impact of detected faults on software reliability. This is the first method of its kind in the literature. Starting from this method, software project stakeholders are allowed to determine at a very early development stage whether or not the project is at high risk of failure while limited information about the software project is available. They can assess the risks of a project and either mitigate the risks before it is too late to do so or cancel the project. This method can be easily adapted to computer processing and automation.

3. Feasibility and scalability assessment of the early-stage reliability prediction approach. This study also addresses the feasibility and scalability aspects of modeling natural languages functional requirements based on the formalized measurement. The nature of the technical barriers on scalability is explored and rule-based methods are developed to overcome these barriers. The impact of the writing style and application type (domain) of the requirements specifications on the effectiveness and efficiency in using the formalized measurement is statistically verified.

Chapter 2: Background and Related Work

2.1 Definitions

Within the software engineering community, there is much inconsistency and confusion over the use of the terms *bug, error, defect, fault, failure, measure, metric,* and *measurement.* Please be aware that this study follows the definitions of IEEE Std. 610.12-1990 [1] and IEEE Std. 1061-1998 [2] when using these terms. It is first necessary to define some of the terms used in this dissertation:

- *Software reliability*: is defined as "the probability of failure-free software operation for a specified period of time in a specified environment" [3]. By this definition, software reliability is a strictly operational quality attribute. Although researchers have come up with models relating the two, software reliability is inherently not a function of time [4].

- *Error*: a human action that produces an incorrect result [1].

- *Fault* (also known as *bug* or *defect*): a flaw in a component or system that can cause the component or system to fail to perform its required function, e.g. an incorrect statement or data definition. A fault is a manifestation of an error in software. A defect, if encountered during execution, may cause a failure of the component or system [1].

- *Failure*: the inability of a system or component to perform its required functions within specified performance requirements [1].

9

The relationship among software error, fault, and failure is illustrated in Figure 2-1.

Figure 2-1: Relationship among the Error, Fault, and Failure

- *Measure*: a way to ascertain or appraise value by comparing it to a norm; to apply a metric [2].

- *Metric*: a quantitative measure of the degree to which a system, component, or process possesses a given attribute [1].

- *Measurement*: the act or process of assigning a number or category to an entity to describe an attribute of that entity; a figure, extent, or amount obtained by measuring [2].

2.2 Current Situation

As revealed in the literature [3][4][5], the cost of a software application in the past decades was sweat, blood, tears, and endless debugging sessions. This is because the demand for complex software systems has increased more rapidly than the ability to design, implement, test, and maintain them. Besides, the ever increasing complexity of software has impaired our ability to understand how faults are born, manifest, propagate, and eventually lead to failures of the software. Many reported system outages or machine crashes were traced down to computer software failures, such as the London Stock Exchange crash in 2008, the Air-Traffic Controller incident at LA

10

Airport in 2004, and the Northeast Blackout in 2003 [6]. As literature is replete with horror stories regarding software problems, the reliability of software systems has become a major concern for our modern society.

Though frustrating, the quest of quantifying software reliability has never ceased. The magnitude of costs involved in software development and maintenance magnifies the need for a scientific foundation to support programming standards and management decisions by measurement. Naturally, software reliability measurement has become essential to quality-assured software engineering [7].

Unfortunately, measuring and ensuring software reliability is no easy task. The high complexity of software is the major contributing factor of software reliability problems [3]. As hard as the problem is, promising progresses are still being made toward more reliable software. More standard components and better process are introduced in the software engineering field. However, until now, we still have no good way of measuring software reliability. Actually, reliability measurement in software is still in its infancy [3]. This is because:

- We do not have a good understanding of the nature of software.
- We cannot find a suitable way to measure software reliability, and most of the aspects related to software reliability.
- Software reliability cannot be directly measured, so other related factors are measured to estimate software reliability and compare it among products. However, even the most obvious product metrics such as software size have not uniform definition.

11

- Even though researchers agree that development process, faults and failures found are all factors related to software reliability, no good quantitative methods have been developed to represent software reliability without excessive limitations.

2.3 Reliability Measurement vs. Development Phases

A software project is made up of series of development phases. Broadly, most software projects are comprised of the following phases [8]:

1. Requirements analysis: This first step is also the most important, because it involves gathering information about what the customer needs and defining, in the clearest possible terms, the problem that the product is expected to solve. Analysis includes understanding the customer's business context and constraints, the functions the product must perform, the performance levels it must adhere to, and the external systems it must be compatible with. Techniques used to obtain this understanding include customer interviews, use cases, and "shopping lists" of software features. The results of the analysis are typically captured in a formal *Software Requirements Specification* document (SRS), which serves as input to the next step. Proper requirements and specifications are critical for having a successful project. Removing faults at this phase can reduce the cost as much as faults found in the Design phase.

2. Design: This step consists of defining the hardware and software architecture, specifying performance and security parameters, designing data storage containers and constraints, choosing the Integrated Development Environment

(IDE) and programming language, and indicating strategies to deal with issues such as exception handling, resource management and interface connectivity. This is also the stage at which user interface design is addressed, including issues relating to navigation and accessibility. The output of this stage is one or more design specifications, which are used in the next stage of implementation.

3. Implementation: This step consists of actually constructing the product as per the design specification(s) developed in the previous step. Typically, this step is performed by a development team consisting of programmers, interface designers and other specialists, using tools such as compilers, debuggers, interpreters and media editors. The output of this step is one or more product components, built according to a pre-defined coding standard and debugged, tested and integrated to satisfy the system architecture requirements.

4. Testing: In this stage, both individual components and the integrated whole are methodically verified to ensure that they are fault-free and fully meet the requirements outlined in the first step. An independent quality assurance team defines "test cases" to evaluate whether the product fully or partially satisfies the requirements outlined in the first step. Three types of testing typically take place: unit testing of individual code modules; system testing of the integrated product; and acceptance testing, formally conducted by or on behalf of the customer. Faults, if found, are logged and feedback provided to the implementation team to enable correction. This is also the stage at which

product documentation, such as a user manual, is prepared, reviewed and published.

5. Operation: This step occurs once the product has been tested and certified as fit for use, and involves preparing the system or product for installation and use at the customer site. Delivery may take place via the Internet or physical media, and the deliverable is typically tagged with a formal revision number to facilitate updates at a later date.

6. Maintenance: This step occurs after installation, and involves making modifications to the system or an individual component to alter attributes or improve performance. These modifications arise either due to change requests initiated by the customer, or faults uncovered during live use of the system. Typically, every change made to the product during the maintenance cycle is recorded and a new product release is performed to enable the customer to gain the benefit of the update.

Measurement of both the product and development processes has long been recognized as a critical activity for successful software development [4]. Good measurement practices and data enable realistic project planning, timely monitoring of project progress and status, identification of project risks, and effective process improvement. Appropriate measurements and indicators of software artifacts such as requirements, designs, and source code can be analyzed to diagnose problems and identify solutions during project execution and reduce faults, rework (effort, resources, etc.), and cycle time. These practices enable organizations to achieve higher quality products and reflect more mature processes, as delineated by the Capability Maturity

Model Integration (CMMI®) [9]. The relationship between software development process and reliability measurement is depicted in Figure 2-2.

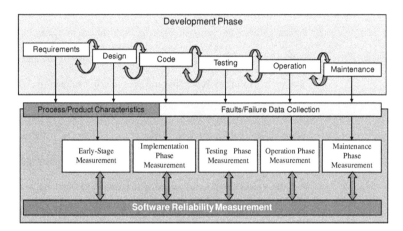

Figure 2-2: Software Reliability Measurement vs. Development Process

2.4 Brief Taxonomy of Software Reliability Measurement Models

The current practices of software reliability measurement include two types of activity: reliability estimation and reliability prediction [3]:

- Reliability estimation: This activity determines current software reliability by applying statistical inference techniques to failure data obtained during system test or during system operation. This is a measure regarding the achieved reliability from the past until the current point. Its main purpose is to assess the current reliability, and determine whether a reliability model is a good fit in retrospect.

15

- Reliability prediction: This activity determines future software reliability based on available software metrics and measures. Depending on the software development stage, prediction involves different techniques:

    o When failure data are available (e.g., software is in system test or operation stage), the estimation techniques can be used to parameterize and verify software reliability models, which can perform future reliability prediction.

    o When failure data are not available (e.g., software is in the design stage), the metrics obtained from the software development process and the characteristics of the resulting product(s) can be used to determine reliability of the software upon testing or delivery. This is usually called "early prediction".

Fenton [10] classified software metrics into three main categories: product, process, and project metrics:

- Product metrics are those that describe characteristics of the software development life cycle processes outputs such as requirements specifications documents, design diagrams, source code, and executable programs. Examples of classical product oriented metrics are McCabe's Cyclomatic Complexity, Line of Code (LOC), and Mean Time To Failure (MTTF) [11][12].

- Process metrics quantify attributes of the development process and of the development environment. Research has demonstrated that a relationship

16

exists between the development process and the ability to complete projects on time and within the desired quality objectives [13]. Higher reliability can be achieved by using better development process, risk management process, configuration management process, etc. Therefore, process metrics, such as the SEI Software CMM level, were also used to estimate, monitor and improve the reliability and quality of software.

- Project metrics are those that describe the available resources characteristics, for instance, the number of developers and their skills. These metric are rarely used in the field of software reliability measurement.

Figure 2-3 shows a brief taxonomy of software reliability models. Most of the existing software reliability models fall in the estimation category.

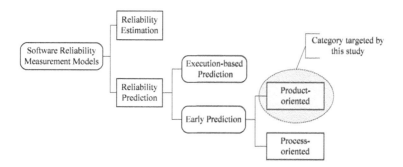

Figure 2-3: Brief Taxonomy of Software Reliability Measurement Models

This study focuses on developing product-based methods for early software reliability measurement.

2.5 Why Early Reliability Measurement is Necessary

Studies support the following claims:

• The majority of software projects fail to achieve schedule and budget goals.

• The majority of faults have their root cause in poorly defined requirements.

• The cost of fixing a software fault is lowest in the requirements phase.

2.5.1 Majority of Software Projects Failed to Achieve Schedule and Budget Goal

Studies describe what has been the industry reality for decades: the majority of software projects failed to achieve schedule and budget goals.

A summary of 1995 Department of Defense (DoD) software spending [14] is shown in Figure 2-4. As indicated, of the $35.7 billion spent by the DoD for software development, only 2 percent of the software was able to be used as delivered. The vast majority, 75 percent, of the software was either never used or was cancelled prior to delivery. The remaining 23 percent of the software was used following modification.

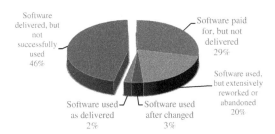

Figure 2-4: Outcomes of Department of Defense Software Spending

18

A similar study conducted by the Standish Group [15] on non-DoD software projects in 1994 produced very similar results. In over 8,000 projects conducted by 350 companies, 28% of projects are failures, 46% are challenged, and only 26 percent of the projects were considered successful.

Poor software quality is a primary factor behind many failures, and often results in massive rework of application scope, design and code [15]. Such rework extends release cycles and consumes significant additional budget. Aside from the time and money spent for application rework and increased help desk support, business reputation and market position can also be compromised. To reduce software failures, it is imperative that we better understand the quality initiatives behind the products being developed for today's global economy.

2.5.2 Requirements are the Root of Many Problems

There is strong evidence that early stages of the system development life cycle are especially prone to faults. Confusion, misunderstanding, and frustration relative to requirements are major risks to the success of any software project.

Inspection statistics for NASA shuttle software showed that the density of major faults found during requirements inspections was seven times higher than during code inspections [16].

In a study of a US Air Force project by Sheldon [17], faults were classified by source. It was found that requirements faults comprised 41% of the faults discovered, while logic design faults made up only 28% of the total fault count.

Other case studies back this result as well. For example, a study by James Martin [18] reported that over half of all project faults could be traced to faults made during

19

the requirements stage as indicated in Figure 2-5 (adapted from [18]). Further, the study stated that approximately 50 percent of requirements faults were the result of poorly written, ambiguous, unclear and incorrect requirements. The other 50 percent of requirements faults could be attributed to incompleteness of specification (i.e. requirements that were simply omitted.)

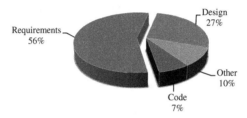

Figure 2-5: Distribution of Faults in Software Projects

Other statistics demonstrated similar problems:

- 70-85 percent of application rework was related to faults in requirements [18]
- 44% of projects were cancelled due to problems with requirements [18]
- 54% of initial project requirements were actually realized [15]
- 45% of realized requirements ended up actually being used [15]

A survey of the Standish Group [15] also found that of the eight main reasons given for project failures, five were requirements related, as presented in Figure 2-6 (adapted from [15]). These were "incomplete requirements", "lack of user involvement", "unrealistic user expectations", "requirements keep changing", and "system no longer needed".

20

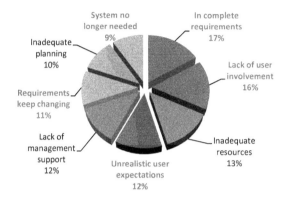

Figure 2-6: Distribution of Failure Causes of 8000+ projects

More recently, an analysis of the data gathered by the Software Engineering Institute (SEI) on 451 Capability Maturity Model (CMM) Level 1 CMM-Based Assessments for Internal Process Improvement conducted from 1997 through August 2001 indicated that requirements continued to be a problem [19].

Getting the requirements right is probably the single most important thing that can be done to achieve customer satisfaction.

2.5.3 Faults Cost Less when Detected and Fixed in Early Stages of Development

The importance of requirements is further emphasized by Figure 2-7 (adapted from [20]), which depicts the distribution of effort needed to fix faults [20]. It can be clearly seen that the bulk of the effort (82%) is attributed to fixing requirement faults.

21

Figure 2-7: Distribution of Effort to Fix Faults

As accepted by the majority of the practitioners, the cost of fixing a software fault is lowest in the requirements phase. As the project moves into subsequent phases of software development, the cost of fixing a fault rises dramatically, since there are more deliverables affected by the correction of each fault, such as a design document or source code. The earlier a fault is detected, the less damage it can do to the system, because there are very few deliverables to correct.

According to the industrial data, the cost of detecting and removing a fault that is introduced during the earlier phases of the software development life cycle increases almost exponentially as we progress through the development life cycle (see Figure 2-8, excerpted from [21]).

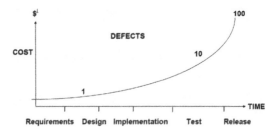

Figure 2-8: Industry Standard Cost Ratio to Fix a Defect

22

McConnell [22] estimated that "a requirements fault that is left undetected until construction or maintenance will cost 50 to 200 times as much to fix as it would have cost to fix at requirements time."

Other studies, furthermore, show that requirements faults are between 10 and 100 times more costly to fix during later phases of the software life cycle than during the requirements phase itself. Let us assign a unit cost of one ("1X") to the effort required to detect and repair a fault during the requirement stage. The same fault, if not found until integration testing or production, will cost hundreds or even thousands of times more (see Figure 2-9, adapted from [13]).

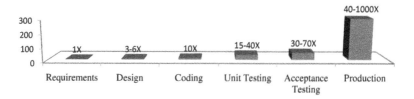

Figure 2-9: Cost Ratio vs. Development Phases in Which Faults are Found

The reason for this large difference is that many of these faults are not detected until well after they have been made. This delay in fault discovery means that the cost to repair includes both the cost to correct the offending fault and the cost to correct subsequent investments in the faults which were made in later phases. These investments include the cost for redesign and replacement of code, cost for documentation rewrite, and the cost to rework or replace software in the field. Indeed, the key issue is scrap and rework. If a fault was introduced while coding, one can just

23

fix the code and re-compile. However, if a fault has its roots in poor requirements and is not discovered until integration testing then one must re-do the requirements, re-do the design, re-do the code, re-do the tests, re-do the user documentation, and re-do the training materials. It is all this "re-do" work that sends projects over budget and over schedule.

This claim is supported by many studies. For instance, in a study performed at Raytheon, Dion [23] reported that approximately 40% of the total project budget was spent in rework costs. Other studies [24] indicate that for the majority of companies today, rework contributes between 30-40% of total project costs. Because of their large number, and the multiplying effect, finding and fixing requirement faults consumes between 70% - 85% of total project rework costs.

Faults are introduced in various stages of the development process, as shown in Figure 2-10 (excerpted from [25]). This figure shows that faults which originate in early stages can have a lasting influence on the quality of a system: they are the earliest to invade the system and the last to leave, if not fixed. This is called "fault summation effect" [25], which explains why requirements faults, in comparison to faults introduced into projects in later development phases are usually more expensive to be defected and fixed.

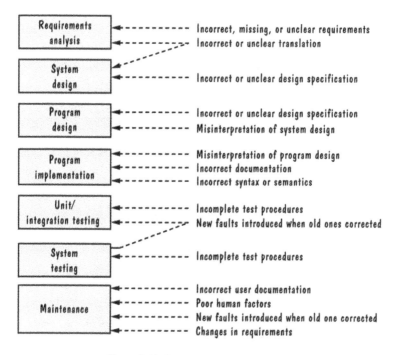

Figure 2-10: Summation Effect of Faults

The role of software has shifted from simply generating financial or other mathematical data to monitoring and controlling equipment which directly affects human life and safety. Software's increasing role creates both requirements for being able to trust it more than before, and for more people to know how much they can trust their software products. As a result, methods used to achieve, predict, and assess the safety and reliability of software are strongly needed in academia, industry, and government. This is also true since many legal issues related to software liability are evolving [26].

Different parts of the software-related industry and society face different challenges. For engineers and managers involved in the development of software systems, there is a strong need for early indicators, such as reliability, so that actions can be taken early to reduce cost and prevent disasters. For regulators and policy makers involved in the certification of software systems, practical methods and tools are needed to quantitatively assess the quality of the software products, including requirements specification, design documents, delivered source code, and user manual [26].

Clearly, current software engineering suffers from problematic requirements specifications. Matured, well-defined, and quantitative assessment methods for the reliability of the software products are not generally applicable until later life cycle phases. Most engineering methods remain qualitative and depend heavily on engineering judgment during the requirements phase. Therefore, the need to develop better software requirements engineering techniques is urgent [16].

2.6 *Virtues of Early Software Reliability Measurement*

First, the advantage for early software reliability measurement is simple economics. Requirements faults are major source of project failures and the most expensive ones to be fixed. Therefore, detection and removal of requirement faults in the early stage of the life cycle will significantly improve the quality of the product in a cost-effective manner. With the cost of some systems exceeding tens or even hundreds of millions of dollars and with development duration of more than 12 to 18 months, early reliability measurement can significantly contribute to the success or early rational cancellation of the project [27].

26

Secondly, early software reliability measurement provides a solid foundation to perform meaningful tradeoff studies at project start. If software reliability measurement is performed early in the software life cycle, it is possible to determine what improvement, if any, can be made to the software methods, techniques, or organizational structure.

Thirdly, with recent strong emphasis on speed of development, the decisions made on the basis of early reliability estimation can have the greatest impact on schedules of software projects [27]. It was observed that early defect detection could significantly shorten the schedule, as shown in Figure 2-11 (Excerpted from [28]). This is because the future rework is minimized if requirements faults are detected and removed during early stages of software development [28].

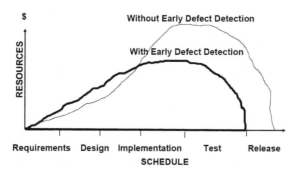

Figure 2-11: Development Schedule with/without Early Fault Detection

2.7 *Previous Work on Early Reliability Measurement*

Early software reliability measurement has attracted great interest from software practitioners and researchers since the early 1990's. However, quantifying software

27

reliability in an early stage has been a difficult research subject that many researchers have attempted to solve with limited success [4].

Traditional software-reliability prediction methods such as reliability growth models base estimates on observing failures (and fixing faults) in validation testing, during which operational patterns represent the product's actual field use. Unfortunately, in early developmental stages of software, failure data is not available to determine the reliability of software. Therefore, although many techniques and models have been developed, only a few can be applied in early development stages, e.g. design phase, before an executable version of the software system is available. This is because only those methods/models that can provide a reasonable estimation without the need of any actual failure data are applicable in early development stages.

The pioneering early-stage reliability measurement models proposed in the early 1990's include: Gaffney and Davis' phase-based model [29], Agresti and Evanco's Ada software defects model [30], and the US Air Force's Rome Lab model [31]. The basic philosophy of these early-phase models is to obtain as much information as possible. This type of approach is referred to as the "white box" approach, which requires detailed information usually not available in most cases. For instance, the US Air Force Rome Lab model consists of nine factors that are used to predict the fault density of the software application. There are parameters in this estimation model that have tradeoff capability (maximum/minimum predicted values). The analyst can determine where some changes can be made in the software engineering process or product to achieve improved fault-density estimation. However, this tradeoff is valuable only if the analyst has knowledge of the software development process.

28

Smidts et al (1997) [32][33] proposed an architecturally based software reliability model to predicting software reliability based on a systematic identification of software process failure modes and their likelihoods. A direct consequence of the approach and its supporting data collection efforts is the identification of weak areas in the software development process. The author believed that the key characteristics of the approach are applicable to other software-development life-cycles & phases. However, it is unclear how difficult the implementation of the approach would be, and how accurate the predictions would be.

Yin et al (2000) [34] addressed early-stage system-level software reliability modeling issues for large-scale software products by taking a hierarchical description and using Petri net mechanisms. The Petri net modeling techniques were proposed for handling the dependency among software modules. This approach requires only a minimum amount of information, which is most likely to be available in early development stages. However, to create a Petri net model for software modules can be fairly complex, especially for large-scale programs.

Zhao (2003) [35] presented software reliability modeling issues in the early stage of a software development for a fault tolerant software management system. Based on Stochastic Reward Nets, a model of the hierarchical view for a fault tolerant software management system is put forward, and an approach that consists of system transient performance analysis was adopted.

Tripathi and Mall (2005) [36] developed a model based on Reliability Block Diagram (RBD) for representing real-world problems and an algorithm for analysis of these models in the early phases of software development. The simulation result

29

shows that reliability prediction of subsystems is a good quality indicator and coupling can be correlated with system reliability, which can be used for system design assessment.

By assuming the same failure rate between two similar projects, Hu (2006) [37] suggested to "reuse" failure data from previous releases or similar projects with ANN models to improve early reliability prediction for current project/release. Better prediction performance was observed in the early phases of testing compared with the original ANN model without failure data reuse.

Mei (2007) [38] investigated an approach to using past fault-related data with Wavelet Networks model to improve reliability predictions in the early testing phase. The wavelet-networks-based model captures the input-output (I/O) relationships of software system to corresponding fault and to improve the accurate of predicting the reliability. Numerical example was illustrated with both actual and simulated datasets. The analysis with example shows that the proposed approach works effectively in the early phase of software testing.

More recently, Cheung et al (2008) [39] presented a framework for predicting reliability of software components during architectural design phase by exploiting architectural models and associated analysis techniques, stochastic modeling approaches, and information sources available early in the development life cycle. The authors agreed that the scalability of their reliability prediction techniques at the system level remains a challenge and further investigation is needed.

Our previous research [40] (to be printed) proposed an approach estimates the fault contents based on data collected by Software Productivity Research Inc. [41]

that links the SEI CMM level to the number of faults per function points. The probability of success per demand is obtained using Musa's exponential model. However, the value of a critical parameter (called fault exposure ratio) in Musa's model was found outdated and incorrect by orders of magnitude in particular for safety critical applications [40].

Common problems with these existing approaches are: lack of generic applicability and scalability, over-dependence on industry-average data, such as faults content per function point, and/or ignorance of product documents generated at early development phase. In particular, Software Requirements Specifications documents (SRS), the most significant documents usually available at the end of requirements phase, are neglected by these approaches due to difficulties in linking requirements-based measurement(s) to reliability. Therefore, they are inevitably unsuited to provide trustworthy results.

Apparently, a new approach is required to bridge the gap between requirements-based measurement(s) and reliability quantification. This probabilistic-reliability prediction approach should also enable software professionals to identify problematic requirements to reduce the risks of software projects.

2.8 *Selecting Software Measurement for Early Reliability Assessment*

There exist more than 200 software measurements [42]. To predict software reliability at the end of the requirements stage with limited information about a system at hand, appropriate measurement(s) need to be selected before methods/models can be developed to bridge the gap between the measurement and the reliability prediction.

31

The desired measurement should possess the following characteristics:

- applicable by the end of the requirements phase;

- involving the use of formal logic and abstract modeling to state the requirements in a clear, precise, and unambiguous format to facilitate the communication among project stakeholders, including domain experts, manager, end users, and developers;

- capable of identifying requirements faults in a systematic way;

- easy to use for all project stakeholders, not just for those with special mathematical training;

- scalable for large/complex applications.

Based on a list of 78 measurements identified in a study conducted by Lawrence Livermore National Laboratory [43], the University of Maryland [12][7] reduced it to 30 (later extended it to 40) and systematically ranked these measurements with respect to their ability at predicting software reliability through expert opinion elicitation process. These measurements were classified into three categories: high-ranked, medium-ranked and low-ranked. This ranking was partially validated through two experiments [40] [44]. Table 2-1 presents the phase-based applicability and ranking classification of these measurements.

In our previous research [40], we found that among the measurements listed in Table 2-1, cause-effect graphing analysis (also called cause-effect graphing) was the most promising candidate and was thereby selected in this study, even though it was ranked as "medium" in the earlier study [12]. The two primary disadvantages keeping it from being widely used in the field of software reliability prediction were [26]:

1) no specific process was defined for the measurement;

2) no method was developed to link this measurement to software reliability.

This study addresses these two primary issues along with others, such as usability

and scalability, to enable software project stakeholders to effectively detect

requirements faults and predict software reliability at the requirements analysis stage.

Table 2-1: Phase-based Applicability and Ranking Classification of 40 Software
Reliability Measurements[1]

| Index | Measure | Applicable Development Phase(s) | | | | Ranking Class |
		Requirement	Design	Implementation	Testing	
1	Bugs per line of code (Gaffney)	✗	✗	✓	✓	Low
2	Cause-effect graphing	✓	✓	✓	✓	Medium
3	Class coupling	✗	✗	✓	✓	Medium
4	Class hierarchy nesting level	✗	✗	✓	✓	Medium
5	Code defect density	✗	✗	✓	✓	High
6	Cohesion	✗	✓	✓	✓	Low
7	Completeness	✓	✓	✓	✓	Low
8	Coverage factor	✗	✓	✓	✓	High
9	Cumulative failure profile	✗	✗	✗	✓	High
10	Cyclomatic complexity	✗	✓	✓	✓	Medium
11	Data flow complexity	✗	✓	✓	✓	Medium
12	Design defect density	✗	✓	✓	✓	High
13	Error distribution	✓	✓	✓	✓	High
14	Failure rate	✗	✗	✗	✓	High
15	Fault density	✓	✓	✓	✓	High

---

[1] Table legend: ✓ = applicable; ✗ = not applicable.

33

Index	Measure	Applicable Development Phase(s)				Ranking Class
		Requirement	Design	Implementation	Testing	
16	Fault-days number	✓	✓	✓	✓	High
17	Feature point analysis	✓	✓	✓	✓	Low
18	Full function point	✓	✓	✓	✓	Low
19	Function point analysis	✓	✓	✓	✓	Low
20	Functional test coverage	✗	✗	✗	✓	Medium
21	Graph-theoretic static architecture complexity	✗	✓	✓	✓	Low
22	Lack of cohesion in methods (LCOM)	✗	✓	✓	✓	Medium
23	Man hours per major defect detected	✗	✗	✗	✓	Medium
24	Mean time to failure	✗	✗	✗	✓	High
25	Minimal unit test case determination	✗	✗	✗	✓	Medium
26	Modular test coverage	✗	✗	✗	✓	Medium
27	Mutation score	✗	✗	✗	✓	Medium
28	Mutation testing (error seeding)	✗	✗	✗	✓	Low
29	Number of children (NOC)	✗	✗	✓	✓	Medium
30	Number of class methods	✗	✗	✓	✓	Medium
31	Number of faults remaining (error seeding)	✓	✓	✓	✓	Medium
32	Number of key classes	✗	✓	✓	✓	Medium
33	Requirements compliance	✓	✓	✓	✓	Low
34	Requirements specification change requests	✓	✓	✓	✓	Medium
35	Requirements traceability	✗	✓	✓	✓	Medium
36	Reviews, inspections and walkthroughs	✓	✓	✓	✓	Medium
37	Software capability maturity model	✓	✓	✓	✓	Medium
38	System design complexity	✗	✓	✓	✓	Medium
39	Test coverage	✗	✗	✗	✓	Medium
40	Weighted method per class WMC)	✗	✗	✓	✓	Medium

Chapter 3: Formalization of Cause-Effect Graphing Analysis as a Software Reliability Measurement

3.1 What is Cause-Effect Graphing Analysis (CEGA)

The Cause-Effect Graphing Analysis technique was originally proposed by Elmendorf [45] to design the necessary and sufficient set of test cases that cover 100 percent of the functional requirements by the use of a mathematically rigorous algorithm. The *Cause-Effect Graphing Analysis* (CEGA) is the process of transforming specifications into a graphical representation, called a cause effect graph. CEGA has a proven beneficial side effect which is to point out incompleteness and ambiguities in specifications as a result of developing cause effect graphs [45][46][47][48].

A *Cause Effect Graph* (CEG) is a visual and formal language into which a natural language specification is translated. More precisely, a CEG is a Boolean graph describing the semantic content of a written functional specification as logical relationships between causes (inputs or stimuli) and effects (outputs). It consists of causes, effects, and graphical notations expressing logical relationships and constraints among causes and effects. The logical operators include "IDENTITY", "AND", "OR", and "NOT". The basic notation for the CEG logical relationships is shown in Figure 3-1.

In most systems, certain combinations of causes are impossible because of syntactic or environmental considerations. To account for these, the notation in

35

Figure 3-2 is used. The *EXCLUSIVE* constraint states that it must always be true that, at most, one of c_1, c_2, ..., and c_k can be "1". The *INCLUSIVE* constraint states that at least one of c_1, c_2, ..., and c_k must always be "1" (c_1, c_2, ..., and c_k cannot be "0" simultaneously). The *ONE-AND-ONLY-ONE* constraint states that one and only one of c_1, c_2, ..., and c_k must be "1". The *REQUIRE* constraint states that for c_1 to be "1", c_2 must be "1" (i.e., it is impossible for c_1 to be "1" and c_2 to be "0"). Besides, there frequently is a need for a constraint among effects. The *MASK* constraint in Figure 3-2 states that if effect e_1 is "1", effect e_2 is forced to "0".

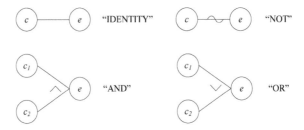

Figure 3-1: Symbols of Basic CEG Logical Relationships

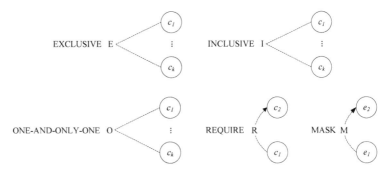

Figure 3-2: Symbols of CEG Constraints

36

In general, the following steps are taken to derive test cases using CEGA [49]:

1) A cause-effect graph is developed on the basis of the requirements specification.

2) The graph is then converted to a decision table (also called "limited-entry decision table").

3) Finally, the decision table is converted to test cases by applying certain rules. This is why CEGA is usually called decision table testing when it is used for test case design.

This study does not discuss how to create test cases using CEGA. Instead, the interested reader is referred to [45] [48][50] for further information.

3.2 Construction of CEG

In general, the following process is used to construct a CEG for a Software Requirements Specifications document (SRS) [45]:

1) Divide the SRS into multiple workable pieces if necessary.

2) Study the SRS to identify causes and effects.

3) Assign a unique name to every cause and effect.

4) Identify all of the expressed and implied logical relationships and constraints among causes and effects.

Several tools that support CEG drawing are commercially available [48]. BenderRBT® [51], for instance, allows project teams to quickly create cause-effect graphs, complete with node relationships and constraints through its add-ons for

Microsoft Office Visio®. When the cause-effect graph is completed, users can invoke BenderRBT® to design test cases based on the requirements depicted in the graph.

Myers [45 pp. 65-88] provided general CEG construction guidelines widely used in industry. However, there are no specific rules found in the literature on how to identify the elements of a CEG from an SRS, including the causes, effects, logical relationships, and constraints. We will revisit the topic of CEG construction in Chapter 7 and present our attempt to address this issue.

3.3 CEGA as a Software Reliability Measurement

CEGA is also recognized as a software reliability measurement. According to [42], CEGA "aids in identifying requirements that are incomplete and ambiguous", and "explores the inputs and expected outputs of a program and identifies the ambiguities", and "once these ambiguities are eliminated, the specifications are considered complete and consistent". The measure of CEGA is defined as:

$$CE(\%) = 100 \times \left(1 - \frac{A_{existing}}{A_{total}} \right),$$

(Eq. 3-1)

where

$CE(\%)$: the cause-effect measure

$A_{existing}$: number of ambiguities in a program remaining to be eliminated

A_{total} : total number of ambiguities identified

The value of the cause-effect measure is scaled between 0 and 1. A score near 1 is considered better than a score near 0. A value near zero indicates a strong need to trace to the suspected ambiguities and make any necessary change(s) in the requirements specifications. As changes are made to the specifications, the incremental measure values can be plotted to show if improvements are being made and how rapidly.

Be aware that the value of the cause-effect measure, *CE(%)*, is subjectively determined. In fact, there is no standard definition for requirements ambiguity. According to Le [52 p. 13], software requirements ambiguities fall into categories of indeterminacy (vagueness and generality), linguistic (lexical, syntactic, and semantic) ambiguity, and software engineering (requirement domain, application domain, system domain, and development) ambiguity. However, there appears to be no single comprehensive definition of ambiguity in the software engineering literature [52 p. 19]. Each of the following definitions highlights only some aspects of ambiguity and omits others:

- IEEE's definition [53]: "An SRS is unambiguous if, and only if, every requirement stated therein has only one interpretation".

- Davis' definition [54]: "Imagine a sentence that is extracted from an SRS, given to ten people who are asked for an interpretation. If there is more than one interpretation, then that sentence is probably ambiguous."

- Schneider, Maritin and Tsai's definition [55]: "An important term, phrase, or sentence essential to an understanding of system behavior has either been left undefined or defined in a way that can cause confusion and misunderstanding. Note that these are not merely language ambiguities such as an uncertain pronoun reference, but ambiguities about the actual system and its behavior."

39

- Gause and Weinberg's definition [56]: "Ambiguity has two sources, missing information and communication errors. Missing information has various reasons. For instance, humans make errors in observation and recall, tend to leave out self-evident and other facts, and generalize incorrectly. A communication error that occurs between the author and the reader is due to general problems in the writing."

- Kamsties's definition [57]: "A requirement is ambiguous if it has multiple interpretations despite the reader's knowledge of the context. It does not matter whether the author unintentionally introduced the ambiguity, but knows what was meant, or she intentionally introduced the ambiguity to include all possible interpretations. The context is important to be taken into account, because a requirements document cannot be expected to be self-contained in a way that an arbitrary naïve reader could understand it."

The definitions together form a complete overview of the current understanding of ambiguity in Software Engineering [52].

Unsurprisingly, the repeatability of the cause-effect measure, $CE(\%)$, is not guaranteed. The subjective or non-subjective factors, such as personal attributes and knowledge, would to some extent affect the inspector's judgment for what is an SRS ambiguity and what is not. Therefore, it is not appropriate to use the cause-effect measure for quantitatively assessing the reliability of a software system.

3.4 Advantages and Disadvantages of CEGA

CEGA is a proven versatile technique for test case design and requirements specification validation. There are several distinct advantages and disadvantages of using CEGA. The general benefits of CEGA when compared to other testing techniques are [45][46][47][48][58][59]:

- ✓ It is a rigorous method for transforming a natural language specification into a formal language specification. The formal characteristics of CEGA guarantee a complete functional coverage not easily found in the state of the practice "ad hoc manner" testing.

- ✓ The test cases generated can be used during all subsequent levels of testing from unit testing to system testing.

- ✓ CEGA begins the process of integration testing. The code modules eventually must integrate with each other. If the requirements that describe these modules cannot integrate, then the code modules cannot be expected to integrate. The cause-effect graph shows the integration of the causes and effects.

- ✓ The starting point for CEGA is the requirements document. The requirements can describe real time systems, events, data driven systems, state transition diagrams, object oriented systems, graphical user interface standards, etc. Any type of logic can be modeled using a CEG.

- ✓ CEGA can also serve as an advance over other informal, ad-hoc specification of program function and combinatorial testing of interfaces.

- ✓ CEGA provides consideration of constraints that application of other testing techniques do not provide.

41

✓ CEGA also has the ability to detect defects that cancel each other out, and the ability to detect defects hidden by other things going right.

When compared to other validation techniques, the benefits of CEGA stem from the fact that it is semi-formally based on a graphics form of propositional logic which gives the user some degree of confidence. This means that CEGA yields additional benefits, among them:

✓ CEGA is helpful for creating unambiguous, concise specifications during requirements phase. CEGs graphically display relationships and constraints between application inputs and outputs. They provide detailed analysis information in a variety of easy-to-read formats. The analyst may get visual clues about missing or incorrect relationships. The project team can analyze every aspect of the requirements in CEGs to identify precedence problems in relations, logical faults, missing functionality and improperly used aliases.

✓ CEGs help to uncover ambiguities and incompleteness in the specification during verification and validation (V&V)[2]. Development of the CEG from the specification allows a thorough inspection of the specification. Any omissions, inaccuracies, or inconsistencies are likely to be detected. In developing cause-effect graphs, project teams evaluate the requirements for completeness, consistency, sufficient level of detail and lack of ambiguity, often finding

---

[2] Verification and Validation (V&V) is the process of checking that a product, service, or system meets specifications and that it fulfills its intended purpose [28]. These are critical components of a quality management system such as ISO 9000.

42

defects that otherwise would not be found until integration testing. Business analysts and project stakeholders collaboratively can review the natural language test cases generated by CEGA, enabling them to identify and correct any requirement faults earlier in the development cycle.

✓ CEGA is easy to use. The only requirement for using and understanding CEG is knowledge of Boolean logical operators.

✓ CEGA is more methodical and therefore more uniform, repeatable, and reliable.

✓ CEGA requires only functional requirements specifications, which is most likely to be available in the early stages of the software development. Therefore, CEGA can be used early in the development process in conjunction with review procedures such as Desk Checking and Walkthroughs [60].

✓ CEGA facilitates early involvement of customers to ensure the application meets their needs. The client's ability to state the right mission goals and needs is essential to attain a requirements specification that is complete, correct and consistent, which in turn is a prerequisite for the right system to be ordered and to enable cost-effective design, verification and validation.

✓ Many aspects of the cause-effect graphing can be automated. For instance, conversion of the graph to a decision table is an algorithmic process, which could be automated by a computer program. This trait implies that CEGA as a testing technique would be scalable for large-scale application.

✓ CEGA improves team communications and reduces risks, rework, and frustration. Requirements definition with visual specifications promotes positive communication. As a visualized representation of requirements, CEG can ease the build of a common understanding between the domain experts, end users, managers, analysts, developers, and test personnel of project needs and commitments. Each project role gains the same understanding of the expected behavior of the software before it is developed, thereby reducing the risk of rework occurring throughout the software development life cycle.

✓ CEGA closes the "language gap" between business and IT and enables the "Big Picture" view of the business by facilitating a more structured dialogue between the two teams. Business stakeholders are often domain experts, speaking the "domain language," but lack understanding of technical terminology. IT stakeholders are well versed with the technical terminology, but often lack expertise and understanding of the problem domain. A CEG synchronizes the two teams by facilitating an accurate and complete "knowledge transfer" from analysts and business stakeholders to the technical team. CEGs provide both nontechnical and technical audiences with a clear and concise understanding of expected system behavior. Their input can be captured and used to iteratively improve and refine the requirements.

✓ CEGA eases compliance with standards and regulations. Validation of requirements using CEGA and testing software using the test cases developed from CEGA satisfy the definition of V&V (validation and verification) in the Capability Maturity Model® Integration^{SM} (CMMI^{SM}) [9].

While there are a number of advantages to using CEGA, there are some disadvantages as well. Researchers and practitioners [26][48][49][50][58][59][61] have observed some common difficulties when using CEGA:

✕ No specific rules are rigorously defined for identifying causes, effects, logical relationships, and constraints, although the general procedure is known. As a result, CEGA has to be performed by domain specialists, people who have expert knowledge of the problems under study. A domain specialist may be a problem owner, an end user of the required system, a sponsor, an outside specialist, a manager, etc.

✕ Complexity of the graph generation task. The main drawback is probably the up-front cost of deriving causes, effects, and constraints from a given informal specification, even if these up-front costs are small compared to the potential major downstream savings because they might avoid unnecessary rework and operational problems.

  – Identifying causes and effects would be very tedious.

  – Identifying the true logical relationship between the causes and the constraints requires domain knowledge.

  – The process of actually drawing the graphs is a very time consuming process even with the help of commercial CEG drawing tools.

  – Graphical depiction could be overwhelming. In particular, developing a CEG can become very complicated when a system has a large number of causes and effects. To keep the complexity under control, intermediate nodes are added to represent logical combinations of

45

several causes. However, an appropriate choice of intermediate nodes is frequently not obvious. The possible complexity of CEGs makes it apparent that tool support is necessary for these time-consuming tasks.

- Difficulty of updating CEGs when the specification changes or when the creator realizes that some information has been overlooked. Any changes that occur in the specification must be translated into corresponding changes in the graph. If new cause(s) are added into CEG, much of its internal structure may have to be redesigned. A simpler intermediate representation can ease the difficulty [61].

- Difficulty of verifying the correctness of requirements specifications. The starting point for CEGA is the requirements document. CEGA is valid only if the natural language specification satisfies the customer's intentions. Thus, if the specification is incorrect one will end up with a set of incorrect test cases. Therefore, one must validate the specification itself before applying CEGA to test case design. However, as the complexity and scope of the modeled behavior increases, the graphs become eventually intractable.

- Perceived inability of CEGs to model situations involving time delays and numerically intensive applications.

Though some ambiguities, incompleteness and difficulties exist in CEGA, the concepts of CEG used in specifying the functional behavior of a system make it attractive from a usability perspective. The CEGA technique is an advance over informal, ad-hoc specifications of systems. It is systematic even though subjective in the first stage of construction of the CEG, and therefore relatively uniform, repeatable,

46

and reliable. It is based on a graphical form of propositional logic, which gives the user some degree of confidence in the specification power of the graph. As a result, CEGA has been widely recognized as a testing technique [60][62].

However, CEGA is not extensively used as a software reliability measurement, even though it potentially provides a very systematic and pretty thorough way of checking the end functionality required by the user. In addition to difficulties mentioned previously, some possible reasons for this lack of interest are:

✕ Repeatability issue. For a measurement to be useful it must be repeatable. When software measurement definitions are incomplete or unspecific, it is easy to collect invalid or incomparable measurement(s) from different data collectors. Thus, the primary issue is not only whether a definition for a measurement is theoretically correct, but also specific enough, such that everyone understands what is to be measured and what the measured values represent. Until then, the values cannot be collected consistently and other people, different from the collectors, can interpret the results correctly and apply them to reach valid conclusions. Our experience with [12] [40] has shown that no standard definition exists that ensures repeatability of the CEGA measurement. To correct this, this study begins by reviewing the definitions of CEGA to define more precise and rigorous measurement rules.

✕ The Cause-effect measure, CE(%), is too undependable to be used as an indicator of software reliability. CE(%) is the ratio of the number of removed ambiguities, $\left(A_{total} - A_{existing} \right)$, to the total number of ambiguities identified in

SRS, A_{total}. The major difficulty of counting ambiguities is that for any specification, there is always some who understand it differently from others. According to our experience [26][40], the values of $A_{existing}$ and A_{total} subjectively depend on the person exercising CEGA. Other factors, such as the level of granularity to which an SRS should be broken up and the writing style of an SRS, can also have a significant influence on the value of CE(%).

These limitations have inevitably kept CEGA from being widely adopted in the field of software reliability engineering. Actually, the CEGA measurement was ranked as "medium" among 40 software reliability measurements by experts with respect to its ability at predicting software reliability [12] (also see Table 2-1). Even worse, CEGA has been removed from IEEE Std. 982.1-2005 [11], the latest edition of IEEE Std.1-1988[42], "IEEE Standard Dictionary of Measures to Produce Reliable Software". The justification of deleting CEGA includes "CEGA is ambiguous", "difficult to interpret", and "its low usage" [11].

To enhance CEGA as a software reliability measurement, this study addresses these limitations by

- Formalizing CEG in terms of mathematics. These formal definitions are necessary to ensure that CEGA is meaningful, true and of known accuracy because without specified rigorous definition and measurement rules, one runs the risk of collecting unrelated, meaningless data. Furthermore, compared to the graphical form of CEG, which is more intuitive and easier to understand, the mathematical form of CEG is far easier to be stored, represented, and

48

implemented by computers, can be updated easily in response to frequent requests for requirements change in practice, and thus has better scalability. This rigorous form of CEG can also serve as an alternative representation of the graphical CEG.

- Investigating rules to ease the task of CEG construction.

- Providing a systematic yet intuitive procedure for applying the proposed CEGA for identifying SRS faults. This further enables a consistent measurement process for CEGA.

- Developing methods for quantifying the impact of identified SRS faults on software reliability. Software faults have different sizes of failure footprints. The impact of a fault on reliability depends on system structure, the way in which a system is used, and location of the fault. Using faults identified in products instead of the aggregated number of faults estimated from empirical data, such as $A_{existing}$, is believed to provide a more solid foundation for reliability quantification [36].

3.5 Formal Definition of CEG

Definition 3-1: CEG

Any *CEG* can be represented by a 4-dimensional tuple where each dimension is a set. Namely,

$$CEG \overset{\text{def}}{=} \langle \hat{C}, \hat{E}, \hat{P}, \overline{CON} \rangle,$$

where

49

$\hat{C} \overset{\text{def}}{=} \{c_i | i = 1,2,\dots,p\}$: is a set of distinct causes, and p is the number of distinct causes.

$\hat{E} \overset{\text{def}}{=} \{e_i | i = 1,2,\dots,q\}$: is a set of effects, and q is the number of effects.

$\hat{F} \overset{\text{def}}{=} \{f_i : \hat{C} \to \hat{E} | i = 1,2,\dots,q\}$: is a set of Boolean functions that map $\hat{C}$ to $\hat{E}$ without applying any constraints. The number of Boolean function is equal to the number of effects.

$\overline{CON} \overset{\text{def}}{=} \{con_i | i = 1,2,\dots,r\}$: is a set of constraints imposed among causes and/or effects , and r is the number of constraints.

Definition 3-2: Cause

A *cause* in a CEG is a primitive input event, typically invoked by a user or external system(s). A primitive input event is an event that cannot be logically expressed by other events. All causes in a CEG are distinct. Redundant causes are not allowed.

A cause has and only has two mutually exclusive states: enabled (represented by "1") or disenabled (represented by "0"). Namely,

$$c = \begin{cases} 1 & \text{if } c \text{ is enabled;} \\ 0 & \text{otherwise.} \end{cases}$$

where c is a cause in a CEG.

Definition 3-3: Effect

An *effect* in a CEG is a system action or output, either observable or non-observable.

In contrast with a cause, an effect must be logically expressed by causes using a Boolean function. Moreover, an effect has and only has three mutually exclusive states: "present"/"triggered" (represented by "1"), "absent"/"non-triggered"

50

(represented by "0"), or "prohibited"/ "not allowed" due to constraint(s) (represented by "NA", which is short for "Not Allowed"). Namely,

$$e = \begin{cases} NA & \text{if any constraint in CEG is applicable;} \\ 1 & \text{if } e \text{ is triggered (determined by its Boolean function);} \\ 0 & \text{if } e \text{ is non-triggered (determined by its Boolean function).} \end{cases}$$

where e is an effect in a CEG.

Definition 3-4: Constraint

A *constraint* in a CEG is a limitation among causes or effects due to syntactic, environmental, or other considerations.

There are five types of constraints used in a CEG. The mathematical symbols and explanation for these constraints are summarized in Table 3-1.

Table 3-1: Mathematical Symbols of CEG Constraints

Constraint Name	Mathematical Symbol	Explanation
EXCLUSIVE	$EXCLUSIVE(c_1, c_2, ..., c_k)$	At most one of the causes among $c_1, c_2, ..., c_k$ can be enabled. This constraint allows simultaneous absence of all of these causes.
INCLUSIVE	$INCLUSIVE(c_1, c_2, ..., c_k)$	At least one of the causes among $c_1, c_2, ..., c_k$ must be enabled. In contrast with the "EXCLUSIVE" constraint, this constraint does NOT allow simultaneous absence of all of these causes.
ONE-AND-ONLY-ONE	$ONE(c_1, c_2, ..., c_k)$	One and only one of the causes among $c_1, c_2, ..., c_k$ can be enabled. This constraint does NOT allow simultaneous absence of all of these causes.
REQUIRE	$REQUIRE(c_1, c_2)$	Cause c_1 cannot be enabled until cause c_2 has been enabled
MASK	$MASK(e_1, e_2)$	The observance of effect e_2 is disguised by effect e_1

51

The following lemmas are helpful when determining if a constraint is applicable to an effect/a given input or not (see Section 5.3.4). The violation of any of these lemmas caused by a constraint indicates the applicability of the constraint to an effect or/and a given input.

Lemma 3-1: EXCLUSIVE Constraint

For a set of causes confined by an EXCLUSIVE constraint, an enabled cause implies that other causes are disenabled. Namely,

$$If\ EXCLUSIVE(c_1, c_2, ..., c_k),\ c_i \Rightarrow \bar{c}_j,\ \forall j \neq i,\ i \leq k,\ j \leq k.$$

Lemma 3-2: INCLUSIVE Constraint

For a set of causes confined by an INCLUSIVE constraint, all causes cannot be disenabled simultaneously. Namely,

$$If\ INCLUSIVE(c_1, c_2, ..., c_k),\ the\ state\ combination\ \bigcap_{i=1}^{k} \bar{c}_i\ is\ not\ allowed.$$

Lemma 3-3: ONE-AND-ONLY-ONE Constraint

For a set of causes confined by a ONE-AND-ONLY-ONE constraint, both the probability of any two different causes being enabled simultaneously and the probability of all causes not being enabled simultaneously are equal to 0. Namely,

$$ONE(c_1, c_2, ..., c_k) \Rightarrow$$
$$\forall i \neq j,\ i \leq k, j \leq k,\ \Pr(c_i \cap c_j) = 0,\ and$$
$$\Pr\left[\bigcap_{i=1}^{k} \bar{c}_i \right] \neq 0.$$

Lemma 3-4: REQUIRE Constraint

52

The implication of constraint cause c_1 requiring cause c_2 is two-fold. First, c_1 cannot be enabled if c_2 has not been enabled yet. Second, c_2 must have been enabled if c_1 is enabled. Namely,

If $REQUIRE(c_1, c_2)$, $\bar{c}_2 \Rightarrow \bar{c}_1$, and $c_1 \Rightarrow c_2$.

Lemma 3-5: Transitive Law for REQUIRE Constraint

The transitive law holds for all *REQUIRE* constraints. Namely,

$$\left.\begin{array}{l} REQUIRE(c_1, c_2) \\ REQUIRE(c_2, c_3) \end{array}\right\} \Rightarrow REQUIRE(c_1, c_3).$$

Lemma 3-6: MASK Constraint

The implication of constraint effect e_1 masking effect e_2 is two-fold. First, e_2 cannot be triggered if e_1 has been triggered already. Second, e_1 is not triggered if e_2 is triggered. Namely,

If $MASK(e_1, e_2)$, $e_1 \Rightarrow \bar{e}_2$, and $e_2 \Rightarrow \bar{e}_1$.

3.6 *Example of CEG Construction*

In this section, we illustrate a sample CEG for a system called LOCAT [63]. LOCAT was designed for a real-time simple projectile tracking system for the Army's all weather Doppler radar system.

For demonstration purpose, only Section 2.1 of LOCAT's SRS was used to construct the sample CEG, as shown in Figure 3-3.

53

...

2 Functional Requirements

2.1 Function Interface

2.1.1 Introduction

Function Interface asks user for the option. The options include: calculation of projection range, calculation of projection speed, calculation of trajectory, and quitting LOCAT. Then the corresponding function is executed.

2.1.2 Inputs

Input is an alphanumeric character specified by the user through the keyboard.

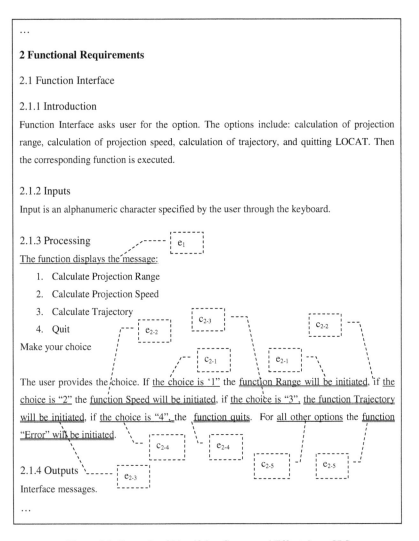

2.1.3 Processing

The function displays the message:

1. Calculate Projection Range
2. Calculate Projection Speed
3. Calculate Trajectory
4. Quit

Make your choice

The user provides the choice. If the choice is '1" the function Range will be initiated, if the choice is "2" the function Speed will be initiated, if the choice is "3", the function Trajectory will be initiated, if the choice is "4", the function quits. For all other options the function "Error" will be initiated.

2.1.4 Outputs

Interface messages.

...

Figure 3-3: Example of Identifying Causes and Effects in an SRS

54

3.6.1 Identified Causes, Effects, Logical Relationships, and Constraints for the Sample SRS

After screening and analyzing the sample SRS, six causes and six effects were identified, as shown in Table 3-2 and Table 3-3, respectively. The first cause in Table 3-2 is inferred from the context of the sample SRS, which is not shown in Figure 3-3. The identified constraints and their explanation are summarized in Table 3-4.

Table 3-2: Identified Causes for the Sample SRS

Cause Index	Explanation	Assigned Identifier
1	The user runs LOCAT.	c_1
2	The user's choice is "1".	c_{2-1}
3	The user's choice is "2".	c_{2-2}
4	The user's choice is "3".	c_{2-3}
5	The user's choice is "4".	c_{2-4}
6	The user's choice is others except "1", "2", "3", and "4".	c_{2-5}

Table 3-3: Identified Effects for the Sample SRS

Effect Index	Explanation	Assigned Identifier
1	Interface message is displayed on the screen to indicate that Function Interface is initiated.	e_1
2	Function Range is initiated.	e_{2-1}
3	Function Speed is initiated.	e_{2-2}
4	Function Trajectory is initiated.	e_{2-3}
5	Function Interface quits.	e_{2-4}
6	Function Error is initiated.	e_{2-5}

55

Table 3-4: Identified Constraints for the Sample SRS

Index	Constraint	Explanation
1	c_{2-1} requires c_1.	The user cannot choose option "1" until LOCAT is initiated.
2	c_{2-2} requires c_1.	The user cannot choose option "2" until LOCAT is initiated.
3	c_{2-3} requires c_1.	The user cannot choose option "3" until LOCAT is initiated.
4	c_{2-4} requires c_1.	The user cannot choose option "4" until LOCAT is initiated.
5	c_{2-5} requires c_1.	The user cannot choose any other option until LOCAT is initiated.
6	c_{2-1}, c_{2-2}, c_{2-3}, c_{2-4}, and c_{2-5} are mutually exclusive.	The user can only choose one option at a time.

3.6.2 Graphical Expression of CEG for the Sample SRS

The figure below shows the CEG constructed for the sample SRS.

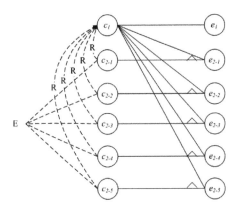

Figure 3-4: Graphical Expression of CEG for the Sample SRS

3.6.3 Mathematical Expression of CEG for the Sample SRS

In contrast with the graphical expression, the following is the mathematical expression of CEG for the sample SRS:

$$CEG_{example} \overset{\text{def}}{=} \langle \hat{C}_{example}, \hat{E}_{example}, \hat{F}_{example}, \widehat{CON}_{example} \rangle,$$

Where

$$\hat{C}_{example} \overset{\text{def}}{=} \{c_1; c_{2\text{-}1}; c_{2\text{-}2}; c_{2\text{-}3}; c_{2\text{-}4}; c_{2\text{-}5}\}$$

$$\hat{E}_{example} \overset{\text{def}}{=} \{e_1; e_{2\text{-}1}; e_{2\text{-}2}; e_{2\text{-}3}; e_{2\text{-}4}; e_{2\text{-}5}\}$$

$$\hat{F}_{example} \overset{\text{def}}{=} \begin{pmatrix} e_1 := c_1; \\ e_{2\text{-}1} := c_1 \cap c_{2\text{-}1}; \\ e_{2\text{-}2} := c_1 \cap c_{2\text{-}2}; \\ e_{2\text{-}3} := c_1 \cap c_{2\text{-}3}; \\ e_{2\text{-}4} := c_1 \cap c_{2\text{-}4}; \\ e_{2\text{-}5} := c_1 \cap c_{2\text{-}5} \end{pmatrix}$$

$$\widehat{CON}_{example} \overset{\text{def}}{=} \begin{Bmatrix} REQUIRE(c_{2\text{-}1}, c_1); \\ REQUIRE(c_{2\text{-}2}, c_1); \\ REQUIRE(c_{2\text{-}3}, c_1); \\ REQUIRE(c_{2\text{-}4}, c_1); \\ EXCLUSIVE(c_{2\text{-}1}, c_{2\text{-}2}, c_{2\text{-}3}, c_{2\text{-}4}, c_{2\text{-}5}) \end{Bmatrix}$$

Figure 3-5: Mathematical Expression of CEG for the Sample SRS

3.7 Summary

This chapter focuses on exploring the advantages and disadvantages of CEGA. Several attempts to enhance CEGA as a scalable software reliability measurement are discussed. Especially, the mathematical expression of CEGs is defined in terms of well understood mathematical entities, such as sets and Boolean formula, whose semantics are formally defined, and can be easily stored and processed by computers. Though informal, unscalable, and unnecessary in our approach, the graphical expression of CEGs helps project stakeholders to find, illustrate, and analyze the software functional requirements, and ease the communication among different project roles. It is desirable to develop a tool that will allow convenient conversion between these two CEG formats.

Chapter 4: Identification of Faults in Software Requirements Specifications Using CEGA

The starting point for CEGA is the Software Requirements Specifications (SRS).

The SRS is the first definitive representation of the capability that the provider is to deliver to the user or acquirer. The SRS becomes the basis for all a project's subsequent management, engineering, and assurance activities. As such, it is a strong source of potential risks that could adversely impact the project's resources, schedules, and products. Because of the criticality of the SRS, it is important to prevent or correct shortcomings in both the form and content of the SRS document before it is established as a project baseline.

Since most of software faults can be traced to faulty functional requirements, it is obvious that the major opportunity for improving the quality of software systems lies in improving the quality of SRS. It would also benefit the entire project team if there is one, clear, detailed, testable set of requirements that they can work from.

Existing SRS quality improvement methods force all SRS analyzers to rely on nonsystematic techniques to search for a wide variety of SRS defects. CEGA is broadly recognized for its ability to detect incomplete and ambiguous requirements. However, there were no specific rules found in the literature on how to use the power of CEGA for SRS faults detection.

The aim of the work described in this chapter is to develop CEGA-based techniques for natural language SRS faults detection.

The *Software Requirements Specification* (SRS) is defined as "a specification for a particular software product, program, or set of programs that performs certain functions in a specific environment" [7]. It is an outcome of the requirement analysis process. A well-designed, well-written SRS accomplishes four major goals:

1) It provides feedback to the customer.

2) It decomposes the problem into component parts

3) It serves as an input to the design specification.

4) It serves as a product validation check.

Usually, SRS is assumed to be a document, although it can be a database or spreadsheet that contains the requirements, or information stored in a commercial requirements management tool. It typically consists of descriptions for functional and non-functional requirements of the future system:

- Functional Requirement: a functional requirement is a requirement defining functions of the system under development

- Non-functional requirement: a non-functional requirement is a requirement characterizing a system property such as expected performance, robustness, usability, maintainability, etc. Non-functional requirements capture business goals/objectives and product quality attributes.

Software requirements are usually expressed in the form of either formal language or natural language. Despite the remarkable advancements in the design of user-acceptable formal languages, the vast majority of SRSs for software projects are still written in plain English (or in other natural languages) due to its flexibility, expressiveness, communicability, and ease of change.

There are several standards proposed for organizing the contents of SRS written in natural language: NASA-STD-2100-91 [64], MIL-STD-498 Section 5.3 [65], ISO/IEC 12207 Section 5.3.2 [66], and IEEE Std. 830-1998 [53], etc. Among them, IEEE Std. 830-1998 [53] is most widely adopted in industry. Several sample SRS outlines are presented in this standard. These sample templates are not standard and are provided to help the user in organizing the requirements specification document and to help him in improving the readability of the document. Figure 4-1 shows a prototype SRS outline recommended by IEEE Std. 830-1998 [53].

Table of Contents
1   Introduction
     1.1   Purpose
     1.2   Scope
     1.3   Definitions, Acronyms, and Abbreviations
     1.4   References
     1.5   Overview
2   General Description
     2.1   Product Perspective
     2.2   Product Functions
     2.3   User Characteristics
     2.4   General Constraints
     2.5   Assumptions and Dependencies
3   Specific Requirements
     3.1   Functional Requirements
            3.1.1   Functional Requirement 1
                     3.1.1.1 Introduction
                     3.1.1.2 Inputs
                     3.1.1.3 Processing
                     3.1.1.4 Outputs
            3.1.2   Functional Requirement 2
         ....
     3.2   External Interface Requirements
            3.2.1   User Interfaces
            3.2.2   Hardware Interfaces
            3.2.3   Software Interfaces
            3.2.4   Communication Interfaces
     3.3   Performance Requirements
     3.4   Design Constraints
            3.4.1   Standards Compliance
            3.4.2   Hardware Limitations
         ....
     3.5   Attributes
            3.5.1   Security
            3.5.2   Maintainability
            ....
     3.6   Other Requirements
            3.6.1   Data Base
            3.6.2   Operations
            3.6.3   Site Adaptation
               ....

Figure 4-1: Prototype Outline of SRS (extracted from IEEE Std. 830-1998 [53])

4.2 Characteristics of a "Good" SRS

There is no standard definition for what is a "good" SRS. Table 4-1 shows the fundamental characteristics of a "good" SRS proposed by Hammer [67].

Table 4-1: Ten Language Quality Characteristics of an SRS (Adapted from [67])

Quality Characteristic	Explanation
Complete	SRS defines precisely all the go-live situations that will be encountered and the system's capability to successfully address them.
Consistent	SRS capability functions and performance levels are compatible, and the required quality features (security, reliability, etc.) do not negate those capability functions. For example, the only electric hedge trimmer that is safe is one that is stored in a box and not connected to any electrical cords or outlets.
Accurate	SRS precisely defines the system's capability in a real-world environment, as well as how it interfaces and interacts with it. This aspect of requirements is a significant problem area for many SRSs.
Modifiable	The logical, hierarchical structure of the SRS should facilitate any necessary modifications (grouping related issues together and separating them from unrelated issues makes the SRS easier to modify).
Ranked	Individual requirements of an SRS are hierarchically arranged according to stability, security, perceived ease/difficulty of implementation, or other parameter that helps in the design of that and subsequent documents.
Testable	An SRS must be stated in such a manner that unambiguous assessment criteria (pass/fail or some quantitative measure) can be derived from the SRS itself.
Traceable	Each requirement in an SRS must be uniquely identified to a source (use case, government requirement, industry standard, etc.)

Quality Characteristic	Explanation
Unambiguous	SRS must contain requirements statements that can be interpreted in one way only. This is another area that creates significant problems for SRS development because of the use of natural language.
Valid	A valid SRS is one in which all parties and project participants can understand, analyze, accept, or approve it. This is one of the main reasons SRSs are written using natural language.
Verifiable	A verifiable SRS is consistent from one level of abstraction to another. Most attributes of a specification are subjective and a conclusive assessment of quality requires a technical review by domain experts. Using indicators of strength and weakness provide some evidence that preferred attributes are or are not present.

4.3 Faults in SRS

In practice, a perfect SRS without any faults is not easy to achieve. Particularly, SRSs written in a natural language are frequently wordy and unstructured, making them vulnerable to ambiguity, incompleteness, or self-contradiction. Figure 4-2 depicts a generic relationship between desired and actually documented specifications, which is commonly seen in practice.

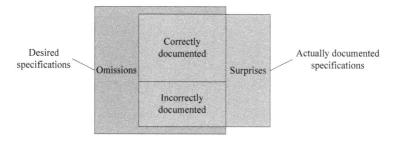

Figure 4-2: Desired vs. Actually Documented Requirements Specifications

An *SRS Fault* is a fault that originates in the requirements phase (e.g., omitted requirement, incomplete requirements description). Typical SRS faults found in practice are:

✗ Noise: the presence of text that carries no relevant information to any feature of the problem.

✗ Silence: a feature that is not covered by any text.

✗ Over-specification: text that describes a feature of the solution, rather than the problem.

✗ Contradiction: text that defines a single feature in a number of incompatible ways.

✗ Ambiguity: text that can be interpreted in at least two different ways.

✗ Forward reference: text that refers to a feature yet to be defined.

✗ Wishful thinking: text that defines a feature that cannot possibly be validated.

✗ Jigsaw puzzles: e.g. distributing requirements across a document and then cross-referencing.

✗ Inconsistent terminology: inventing and then changing terminology.

A more thorough taxonomy of SRS faults was defined by Hays [68], as presented in Table 4-2.

Table 4-2: Taxonomy of SRS Faults (Excerpted from [68])

Major Fault	Sub-faults	Description of Sub-Faults
Incompleteness	Incomplete functional Decomposition	Failure to adequately decompose a more abstract specification.

Major Fault	Sub-faults	Description of Sub-Faults
	Incomplete Functional Description	Failure to fully describe all requirements of a function.
Omitted/Missing	Omitted functional Requirement	Failure to specify one or more of the next lower levels of abstraction of a higher level specified.
	Missing External Constants	Specification of a Missing value or variable in a requirement.
	Missing Description of Initial System State	Failure to specify the initial system state, when that state is not equal to 0.
Incorrect	Incorrect External Constants	Specification of an incorrect value or variable in a requirement.
	Incorrect Input or Output Descriptions	Failure to fully describe system input or output.
	Incorrect Description of Initial System State	Failure to specify the initial system state, when that state is not equal to 0
	Incorrect Assignment of Resources	Over-or-under stating the computing resources assigned to a specification.
Ambiguous	Improper Translation	Failure to carry detailed requirement through decomposition process, resulting in ambiguity in the specification.
	Lack of Clarity	Difficult to understand or lack of clarity and therefore ambiguous.
Infeasible	(None)	Requirement, which is unfeasible or impossible to achieve given other system factors, e.g., process speed, memory available.
Inconsistent	Internal Conflicts	Requirements that are pair-wise incompatible.
	External Conflicts	Requirements of cooperating systems, or parent/embedded systems, which taken pair-wise are incompatible.
Over-specification	(None)	Requirements or specification limits that are excessive for the operational need, causing additional system cost.
Not Traceable	(None)	Requirement which cannot be traced to previous or subsequent phases.
Unachievable Item	(None)	The functional description cannot be true in the reasonable lifetime of the product.
Non-Verifiable	(None)	The requirement description cannot be verified by any reasonable testing methods.
Misplace	(None)	Information which is in a different section in requirements document.
International Deviation	(None)	The Requirement that is specified at higher level but intentionally deviated at lower level from specifications.
Redundant or Duplicate	(None)	Requirement was already specified elsewhere in the specification

65

The study of Hays [68] reported an empirical categorization percentage data, as illustrated in Figure 4-3. The top three categories accounted for almost 80% of the requirement faults evaluated. These three fault categories and their percentages were: Incompleteness (21%), Omitted/Missing (33%), and Incorrect (24%). Most of these faults were related to functional requirements.

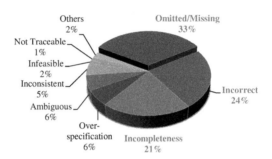

Figure 4-3: Requirements Fault Categorization Percentage Data

4.4 V&V Techniques for SRS Faults Detection

The quality of SRS can be improved and costs and risks can be controlled by performing Verification &Validation (V&V) early in the development process. According to IEEE Std. 1012-2004 [69], Software Verification and Validation (V&V) is the process of ensuring that software being developed or changed will satisfy functional and other requirements (validation) and each step in the process of building the software yields the right products (verification). The main V&V techniques for SRS faults detection are:

• Inspection: SRS Inspection involves a team of people, led by a leader, which formally reviews the SRS. The SRS is presented in front of the inspection team.

The bugs that are detected during the inspection are communicated to the next level in order to take care of them. The objective of an SRS inspection is to detect and identify defects. An SRS inspection is a rigorous peer examination that:

- o identifies nonconformance with respect to specifications and standards;
- o uses metrics to monitor progress;
- o ignores stylistic issues;
- o does not discuss solutions.

- Walkthroughs: Walkthroughs can be considered similar to inspections without the formal preparation (of any presentation or documentations) aspect. During the walkthrough meeting, the presenter/author introduces the material to all the participants in order to make them familiar with it. Even though the walkthroughs can help in finding potential bugs, they are used for knowledge sharing or communication purpose. An SRS walkthrough should attempt to identify defects and consider possible solutions. In contrast with other forms of review, secondary objectives are to educate, and to resolve stylistic problems.

- Technical reviews: The objective of an SRS technical review is to evaluate the SRS, and provide management with evidence that:

- o the SRS has been produced according to the project standards and procedures;
- o changes have been properly implemented, and affect only those system areas identified by the change specification.

- Buddy checks: This is the simplest type of review activity used to find out bugs in an SRS. In a buddy check, one person goes through the SRS prepared by another person in order to find out bugs which the author couldn't find previously.

67

Software inspection is one of the best practices for detecting and removing defects early in the software development process. In a software inspection, review is first performed individually by several reviewers to analyze all or part of the specifications and search for defects, and then by a meeting of the reviewers and author(s) to collect defects. Usually, reviewers use Ad Hoc, Checklist-Based Reading (CBR), or Perspective-Based Reading (PBR) methods to uncover defects. These methods force all reviewers to rely on nonsystematic techniques to search for a wide variety of SRS defects.

4.5 CEGA-based Techniques for SRS Faults Detection

A problem arising in existing techniques mentioned previously is "how to systematically cover requirements (especially functional requirements)", or "what actions have to be taken to ensure a review completely and adequately covers all the requirements called for by users and producers?" According to the analysis in Chapter 3, CEGA might be a good answer to this question.

CEGA is broadly recognized by its ability to "aid[s] in identifying requirements that are incomplete and ambiguous" [42]. However, there have been no specific rules found in the literature on how to use the power of CEGA for SRS faults detection. Addressing to this issue, we proposed a CEGA-based approach for practitioners to detect faults in SRS.

Our approach consists of a two-step process. The initial step includes CEG construction and an optional ambiguity review, which is performed by someone who is not a domain expert. This step takes place after the SRS reaches first draft. In this step, the SRS analyst is not reading the requirements for content, but only to identify

68

ambiguities in the logic and structure of the wording. This review finds all of the generic ambiguities such as unclear references. Since the initial reviewer is not a domain expert they cannot read into the specification facts that are not explicitly there.

Once the issues identified in the initial ambiguity review have been addressed, the requirement is then reviewed for content (i.e., correctness and completeness) by domain experts using the CEG validation algorithm and the related rules.

4.5.1 CEGA-based SRS Faults Taxonomy

CEG is a model to capture the functional requirements specified in an SRS. In other words, a CEG should "faithfully" (to the best knowledge of its constructor(s)) represent the functional requirements stated in an SRS, no matter whether they contain faults or not. When   the functional requirements are translated into a CEG, the faults contained in these requirements should be "mapped" into the CEG as well. These faults fall into one or more of the following fault categories in terms of the CEG:

1) Missing Effect;

2) Extra Effect;

3) Missing Constraint;

4) Extra Constraint;

5) Wrong Boolean Function, including:

   i. Wrong-Boolean-Function Case 1: Missing cause(s) in a Boolean function;

   ii. Wrong-Boolean-Function Case 2: Extra cause(s) in a Boolean function;

   iii. Wrong-Boolean-Function Case 3: Wrong Boolean operator(s) in a Boolean function.

69

The description of the faults categories is summarized in Table 4-3.

Table 4-3: Categories of SRS Faults in Terms of CEG

Fault Category	Description
Missing-Effect	Omission of an effect in CEG.
Extra-Effect	Introduction of an effect that is not desired in CEG.
Missing-Constraint	Omission of a constraint in CEG.
Extra-Constraint	Introduction of a constraint that is not desired in CEG.
Wrong-Boolean-Function Case 1: Missing-cause	Omission of at least a cause in the expression of a Boolean function.
Wrong-Boolean-Function Case 2: Extra-cause	Introduction of at least a cause into the expression of a Boolean function.
Wrong-Boolean-Function Case 3: Wrong-Boolean-operator	Incorrect use of at least a Boolean logic operator in the expression of a Boolean function.

4.5.2 Detecting SRS Faults by CEG Construction and Optional Ambiguities Review

CEGA consists of a manual step of transforming an SRS into a CEG, a more concise and structured representation. The transformation process itself is a form of inspection. For example, the CEG tends to force awareness of the "Else" conditions that weren't explicitly articulated in the structured English. We will revisit the topic on detecting SRS faults during CEG construction in Chapter 7.

According to our experience, the following SRS faults are usually found when constructing CEG:

- Ambiguities: functional requirements which are difficult to understand or lack clarity, such as ambiguous statements caused by implicit connectors or

70

precedence of relation, ambiguous boundary, ambiguous scope of negation, and ambiguous reference.

- Redundancies: requirements that were already specified elsewhere in the specification, such as unnecessary aliases.
- Inconsistencies: pair-wise incompatible functional requirements.
- Incompleteness: failure to fully describe all requirements of a function.

Optionally, a technique called Ambiguity Review can be applied to eliminate potential ambiguities in an SRS prior to the review of requirements for content by the domain experts. An *Ambiguity Review* is a test of an SRS to insure that requirements are written in a clear, concise and unambiguous manner. The intent of the Ambiguity Review is to provide the domain experts with a better quality set of requirements to work from, so they can better identify missing requirements, and improve the content (completeness and accuracy) of all requirements. After the ambiguities are identified, it is the responsibility of the requirements author to correct the ambiguities, and then have the domain experts review the requirements for content.

BenderRBT® Inc. [70] developed an Ambiguity Review technique. The key of this technique is to define a review checklist of 15 ambiguity problems commonly found in an SRS. Many ambiguities referred to in the Ambiguity Review Checklist items can be identified by looking for key words and phrases in the requirements. The list of words pointing to potential ambiguities is given in Appendix A (adapted from [70]).

Ambiguity Review improves the quality of requirements so that the domain experts have a better quality document to work from, and help them make whatever changes are needed to the requirements content, so that requirements are not missed.

It should be noted that CEG construction and ambiguities review can usually detect simple linguistic faults. Other methods/techniques such as CEG validation are needed for detecting implicit faults in an SRS.

4.5.3 Detecting More Implicit SRS Faults by CEG Validation

Validating a CEG consists of checking for the existence of the types of CEG faults mentioned previously in Section 4.5.1. Domain knowledge is needed to perform CEG validation.

The suggested procedure for CEG validation is shown in Figure 4-4. The detailed rules for identifying each type of faults are listed in the following, which were also summarized in our previous research [40] (to be printed).

4.5.3.1. Rules for Identifying Missing Effect(s) in CEG:

The knowledge required to identify missing effects is hard to define since some missing effects are obvious while others are obscure. Generally, the mastery of the operation mechanism of the system is required to find an obscure missing effect.

There is no way to give a concrete process or rule for identifying missing effects.

4.5.3.2. Rules for Identifying Extra Effect(s) in CEG

To identify extra effects, the inspector should be capable of understanding the physical meaning of the effect and determining whether the effect is necessary or not. An unnecessary effect is an extra effect.

72

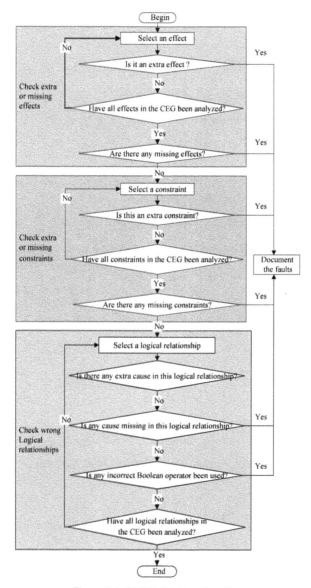

Figure 4-4: CEG Validation Algorithm

73

4.5.3.3. Rules for Identifying Missing Constraint(s) in CEG

To identify missing constraints, the inspector should be capable of understanding the physical meaning of all causes and effects and determining whether any constraint is required to confine these causes/effects or not.

The process for identifying missing constraints is:

1) Arrange all causes in a time sequence.

2) If two cause events occur in a sequential manner, the "REQUIRE" constraint should have been applied to them. If not, it is a missing constraint.

3) For those causes that occur simultaneously, examine whether "EXCLUSIVE", "INCLUSIVE", or "ONE-AND-ONLY-ONE" constraints might have been missed.

4) Arrange all effects in a time sequence.

5) For those effects that can occur simultaneously, examine whether there is any risk for their co-existence. If so, the "MASK" constraint should have been applied to them. If not, it is a missing constraint.

4.5.3.4. Rules for Identifying Extra Constraint(s) in CEG

To identify extra constraints, the inspector should be capable of understanding the physical meaning of all causes or effects in a constraint and determining whether the constraint is necessary or not.

The process for identifying extra constraints is:

1) Arrange all causes in a time sequence.

2) If two cause events do not occur in a sequential manner, the "REQUIRE" constraint should not be applied to them. If applied, it is an extra constraint.

74

3) If two or more events do not occur simultaneously, "EXCLUSIVE", "INCLUSIVE" or "ONE-AND-ONLY-ONE" constraints should not be applied to them. If applied, it is an extra constraint.

4) Examine the "MASK" constraints one by one and determine if each is necessary or not. If not, it is an extra constraint.

4.5.3.5. Rules for Identifying Wrong Boolean Function(s) in CEG

To identify a wrong Boolean function, the inspector should be capable of understanding the physical meaning of all causes or effects. In addition, the inspector should have mastered the operation mechanism of the system to determine what logical relationships should be applied to the causes.

The process for identifying extra constraints is:

1) Consider one Boolean function at a time.

2) Check the causes in the Boolean function one-by-one and determine whether a cause is necessary or not. An unnecessary cause is an extra cause in a Boolean function.

3) Consider the remaining causes in the CEG. If any cause should have been involved in the Boolean function, it is a missing cause.

4) Consider other possible causes not included in the CEG. If any cause should have been involved in the Boolean function, it is a missing cause.

5) Check all Boolean operators in the Boolean function to identify incorrect one(s).

4.6 Summary

The SRS is a model of what the user wants. A consistent, complete, precise, and understandable SRS is the basic premise for the product lifecycle activities, such as analysis, design, coding, testing, use, and maintenance. A software program might be unreliable if it is an implementation of an imperfect SRS. Especially, ambiguous requirements will not yield a satisfactory final product and will likely lead to cost overruns, extended schedules, and missed deliverable deadlines.

In recent years, many semiformal and formal languages such as UML [71], Z-Notation [72], and B-Method [73] have been developed in an attempt to reduce ambiguity, inconsistency, and incorrectness in requirements descriptions. A drawback to these languages, however, is that they are difficult for non-experts to understand, which limits their practical application. Natural language, despite its inherent ambiguity, continues to be the most common way to express software requirements because natural language SRSs can be shared easily among various people involved in the software development process and used in several product development phases.

Empirical studies, such as [74], indicate that the overall SRS inspection performance can be improved when individual reviewers use systematic procedures to address to a small set of specific issues. This contrasts with the usual practice, in which reviewers have neither systematic procedure nor clearly defined responsibilities. The disciplined methods proposed in this chapter can be used for the systematical analysis of natural language SRS and the detection of SRS faults.

4.6.1 Advantages of our Methods

Existing techniques used for natural language SRS fault detection fail to ensure a complete and adequate coverage of all functional requirements specified in an SRS. Our approach distinguishes itself from other SRS fault detection methods by its CEGA-based attribute, which is rigid, systematic, and with 100 percent coverage of functional requirements.

Using our CEGA-based methods, faults residing in an SRS can be detected not only by CEG construction and an optional ambiguity review, but also by systematically validating the constructed CEG.

Compared with commonly used SRS reading techniques, such as ad hoc, and checklist-based reading techniques, our approach provides a more systematic and clearer path for inspectors to follow. This is because CEG is uniform, repeatable, and reliable (when CEG is expressed in mathematical form), and gives a better way for people to communicate (when CEG is expressed in graphical form).

Realistically, one cannot expect to identify types of SRS faults that he or she never ever has thought about or come across. The contribution of our approach (in particular, the CEGA-based SRS faults taxonomy) lies in providing a systematic way to explore this implicitly existing knowledge by using heuristics and in increasing the requirements engineer's awareness of the problematic areas in an SRS.

4.6.2 Limitations of our Methods

Similar to other reading methods, the effectiveness of our approach highly depends on the inspector's knowledge of the system. The more he/she knows the system, the higher the probability that he/she finds fault(s) in an SRS. Any relevant

77

resources, such as the user specification document, an end-user, an analyst and so on, help the inspector improve his/her understanding of the system and identify fault(s) in a CEG. Training is also helpful.

Besides, CEG construction, ambiguity review, and CEG validation are carried out by human reviewers who read SRSs, look for faults, and document the results. The clerical activities are boring, time consuming, and often ineffective. It is desirable to develop an automated tool which

- allows requirements engineers to perform an initial parsing of requirements by automatically detecting potential linguistic defects that can cause ambiguity problems at later stages of software product development.

- extracts structured information and metrics for detecting linguistic inaccuracies and defects

- provides support for the consistency and completeness analysis of the requirements.

Chapter 5: Quantification of the Impact of Faults on Software Reliability

Knowing that software is sufficiently reliable is necessary before we can make intelligent decisions about its use. This is clear for safety-critical and mission-critical systems, where we need to be sure that software failures will not incur unacceptable loss of human life. It is less clear, but also important, in more mundane applications where it must be decided whether the trade-off between new functionality and possible loss of reliability is cost-effective.

Quantification of software reliability can help organizations make informative decisions about corrective actions, about their ability to stay on target, and reach goals. This chapter describes techniques proposed for quantifying software reliability on the basis of CEGA.

Since the value of the cause-effect measure, CE(%), is subjectively determined and using faults identified in products instead of the aggregated number of faults is believed to provide a more solid foundation for reliability quantification [40], our reliability quantification method is based on the faults identified in SRS during the CEGA measurement, but not on the value of CE(%) obtained from the CEGA measurement.

5.1 *Basic Notations and Definitions*

The following notations are used throughout the remainder of this dissertation:

79

A-CEG   =   Actually-implemented Cause Effect Graph, constructed from SRS

B-CEG   =   Benchmark Cause Effect Graph, constructed by removing all identified faults in A-CEG.

$\hat{C}^A$ =   the cause set of A-CEG

$\hat{E}^A$ =   the effect set of A-CEG

$\hat{F}^A$ =   the Boolean function set of A-CEG

$\widehat{CON}^A$ =   the constraint set of A-CEG

$\hat{C}^B$ =   the cause set of B-CEG

$\hat{E}^B$ =   the effect set of B-CEG

$\hat{F}^B$ =   the Boolean function set of B-CEG

$\widehat{CON}^B$ =   the constraint set of B-CEG

e_j^A =   the jth effect in A-CEG. $e_j^A \in E^A$, $j = 1,2,\ldots,m$.

m =   the number of distinct effects in $\hat{E}^A$. This is also the number of distinct effects in $\hat{E}^B$.

e_j^B =   the peer effect in B-CEG corresponding to e_j^A.

n =   the number of distinct causes in $\hat{C}^A \cup \hat{C}^B$

f_j^A =   a Boolean function in F^A corresponding to e_j^A.

f_j^B =   a Boolean function[3] in F^B corresponding to e_j^B.

---

[3] In mathematics, a *Boolean function* is a function of the form f : $\mathbf{B}^k \rightarrow \mathbf{B}$, where $\mathbf{B} = \{0, 1\}$ is a *Boolean domain* and k is a nonnegative integer called the arity of the function.

$\overline{X}$ = a state combination of all distinct causes in

$\hat{C}^A \cup \hat{C}^B$. $\overline{X} = (c_1, c_2, \ldots, c_n)$, where

$$c_i = \begin{cases} 1 & \text{if the } i^{th} \text{ cause is enabled;} \\ 0 & \text{otherwise,} \end{cases} \quad i = 1, 2, \cdots, \text{n}.$$

$\overline{X}^k$ = the kth state combination of all distinct causes in

$\hat{C}^A \cup \hat{C}^B$. $k = 1, 2, \cdots, 2^n$, and $\overline{X}^k = (c_1^k, \ldots c_i^k, \ldots, c_n^k)$,

$$\text{where } c_i^k = \begin{cases} 1 & \text{if the } i^{th} \text{ cause is enabled;} \\ 0 & \text{otherwise,} \end{cases} \quad i = 1, 2, \cdots, \text{n}.$$

Definition 5-1: Input

An input in this study refers to a combination of states of all causes in either A-CEG or B-CEG.

Because any cause can take only two values of either "0" or "1", there are 2^n inputs for a given pair of A-CEG and B-CEG, where n is the total number of distinct causes in the input space $\hat{C}^A \cup \hat{C}^B$.

Any input falls into one of two mutual exclusive categories: failure-relevant and failure-irrelevant.

Definition 5-2: Failure-relevant input

A *failure-relevant input* is such an input that there exists at least an effect in A-CEG, whose outcome in response to this input is different from that of its counterpart in B-CEG.

Definition 5-3: Failure-irrelevant input

In contrast with failure-relevant inputs, a *failure-relevant input* is such an input

81

that outputs of all effects in A-CEG against this input are identical to those of their counterparts in B-CEG.

Definition 5-4: Failure of A-CEG

In software testing, a software system is said to "fail" for a given input if one of the system's actual outputs is in disagreement with expectation. Similarly, a system represented by an A-CEG *fails* if one or more effects in the A-CEG behave differently from expectation for a given input.

5.2 Fundamental Lemma and Overall Algorithm for Quantifying Software Reliability

Lemma 5-1: Fundamental Lemma

Given an A-CEG, the failure probability of a software system is equivalent to the occurrence probability of all failure-relevant inputs. Namely,

$$\text{Probability}(system\ fails) = \text{Probability}\left(failure\text{-}relevant\ inputs\right) \qquad \text{(Eq. 5-1)}$$

Prove:

We may infer from the definitions of *failure-relevant input* and *failure-irrelevant input* that

$$\left(failure\text{-}relevant\ inputs\right) \cup \left(failure\text{-}irrelevant\ inputs\right) = \Omega\ (universal\ set), \text{ and}$$

$$\left(failure\text{-}relevant\ inputs\right) \cap \left(failure\text{-}irrelevant\ inputs\right) = \Phi\ (empty\ set).$$

According to the Law of Total Probability [75 p. 159], we have

82

$$\text{Probability}(\textit{system fails}) = \text{Probability}\left(\textit{system fails}\,|\,\textit{failure-relevant inputs}\right)$$
$$\times\text{Probability}\left(\textit{failure - relevant inputs}\right)$$
$$+\text{Probability}\left(\textit{system fails}\,|\,\textit{failure-irrelevant inputs}\right)$$
$$\times\text{Probability}\left(\textit{failure-irrelevant inputs}\right).$$

(Eq. 5-2)

Moreover, we may also infer from the definitions of *failure-relevant input* and

failure-irrelevant input that

$\text{Probability}\left(\textit{system fails}\,|\,\textit{failure-relevant inputs}\right) = 1$, and

$\text{Probability}\left(\textit{system fails}\,|\,\textit{failure-irrelevant inputs}\right) = 0$.

Therefore, the equation (Eq. 5-2) turns out to be

$$\text{Probability}(\textit{system fails}) = 1\times\text{Probability}\left(\textit{failure-relevant inputs}\right)$$
$$+0\times\text{Probability}\left(\textit{failure-irrelevant inputs}\right)$$
$$= \text{Probability}\left(\textit{failure-relevant inputs}\right).$$

Lemma 5-1 indicates that quantifying a system's failure probability is equivalent

to performing the following two sub-tasks:

1) Determining failure-relevant inputs.

2) Calculating the occurrence probability of all failure-relevant inputs.

Determining failure-relevant inputs can be achieved by examining all possible

inputs, one input at a time, and comparing the actual outputs of effects to the expected

outputs for a given input. However, generating expected outputs for all inputs is non-

trivial. Since there are as many as 2^n inputs (n is the number of causes), the use of a

human expert to create all expected outputs is not only difficult, time-consuming, and

83

non-scalable, but also very error-prone. To aid this task, two concepts, *B-CEG* and *virtual effect*, are introduced in this study. The use of B-CEG and virtual effects are the two pillars of the proposed reliability quantification algorithm. Details about these two concepts are given in Section 5.3.1 and Section 5.3.3, respectively.

The task of calculating the occurrence probability of all failure-relevant inputs is accomplished by employing the BDD techniques to represent the Boolean logic of all relevant inputs and applying a recursive algorithm to calculate the probability of a BDD's top node, as further discussed in Section 5.3.4.

The overall algorithm for predicting software reliability is shown in Figure 5-1.

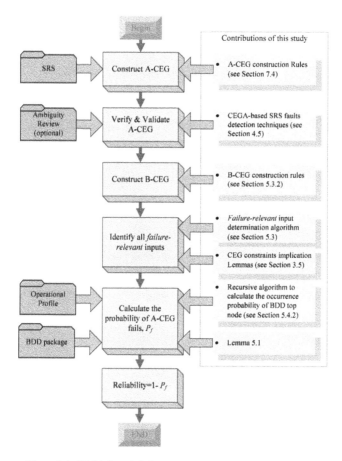

Figure 5-1: CEGA-based Software Reliability Prediction Algorithm

5.3 *Determination of Failure-relevant Inputs*

5.3.1 Introduction of B-CEG

The idea of using B-CEG for failure-relevant inputs identification was inspired by software testing automation. In software testing, the mechanism used to generate

85

expected results is called an *oracle*. An *oracle* is any program, process, or data that provides the test designer with the expected result of a test [62]. The oracle provides the ability to automatically determine whether tests have passed or failed. Typical oracles are [76]:

- Manual verification of results (human "eye-ball" oracle)

- Separate program implementing the same algorithm

- Simulator of the software system to produce parallel results

- Debugged hardware simulator to emulate hardware and software operations

- Earlier version of the software

- Check of specific values for known responses

The use of test oracle in software testing is depicted in Figure 5-2. The test oracle is usually costly and difficult to create.

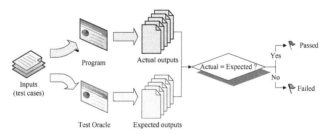

Figure 5-2: Software Testing Using Test Oracle

Similarly, we introduce an artifact, called *Benchmark Cause-Effect-Graph* (*B-CEG*), to facilitate the process of distinguishing failure-relevant from failure-irrelevant inputs. A B-CEG is a "faultless" CEG to the best knowledge of SRS analyst(s). It is "closer" than A-CEG to the O-CEG (*Oracle Cause-Effect Graph*), a

86

"perfect" CEG representing the desired system (refer to Figure 4-2), which is very hard to obtain in practice as pointed out in many studies.

Analogous to a test oracle, B-CEG enables the automation of distinguishing failure-relevant inputs from failure-irrelevant. The use of B-CEG for identifying failure-relevant inputs is depicted in Figure 5-3.

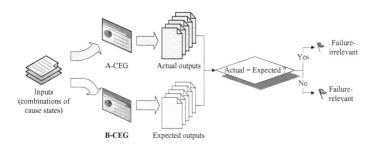

Figure 5-3: Identifying Failure-relevant Inputs Using B-CEG

B-CEG could be constructed either from scratch (called *"addition approach"*) or by making a copy of A-CEG and then rectifying all identified faults (called *"subtraction approach"*). In most cases, the "subtraction approach" is far more efficient than the "addition approach" since there are usually only a few faults in A-CEG. To ease the task of BCEG construction, we developed a set of rules (described in Section 5.3.2) for the "subtraction approach". By following these rules one can easily construct a B-CEG provided that an A-CEG and the faults in the A-CEG are known.

5.3.2 Rules for B-CEG Construction and A-CEG Revision

Similar to an A-CEG, a B-CEG is defined by four sets: a cause set $\widehat{C}^B$, an effect set $\widehat{E}^B$, a Boolean function set $\widehat{F}^B$, and a constraint set $\widetilde{CON}^B$. A B-CEG is determined if and only all of these four sets are determined.

To ease the task of BCEG construction, we developed the rules for determining these four sets, as described below.

5.3.2.1. Determination of $\widehat{C}^B$

The process for determining $\widehat{C}^B$ is:

1) Put all causes in $\widehat{C}^A$ into $\widehat{C}^B$.

2) If a cause does not appear in $\widehat{F}^B$, remove this cause from $\widehat{C}^B$.

3) If a cause does not appear in $\widehat{F}^A$ and appears in $\widehat{F}^B$, add this cause into $\widehat{C}^B$.

5.3.2.2. Determination of $\widehat{E}^B$

The process for determining $\widehat{E}^B$ is:

1) Put all effects in $\widehat{E}^A$ into $\widehat{E}^B$.

2) If there are any detected "introduction-of-an-undesired-effect" faults in A-CEG, for each of these extra effects, update the corresponding Boolean function in $\widehat{F}^B$ such that it always yields "0" for any given input. All of these extra effects are virtual effects in B-CEG.

88

All extra effects are intentionally left in B-CEG. As such, each of extra effects in A-CEG has its counterpart in B-CEG.

3) If there are any detected "missing-an-effect" faults in A-CEG, for each of these missing effects,

    i.   add a new effect identifier into $\widehat{E}^B$.

    ii.   add an appropriate Boolean function into $\widehat{F}^B$.

    iii.   add an effect identifier (identical to its counterpart in B-CEG) into $\widehat{E}^A$. This is a virtual effect in A-CEG. As such, the missing effect in A-CEG has its counterpart in B-CEG.

5.3.2.3. Determination of $\widehat{F}^B$

The process for determining $\widehat{F}^B$ is:

1) Put only those Boolean functions of $\widehat{F}^A$ that are not corresponding to any virtual effects in $\widehat{E}^A$ into $\widehat{F}^B$.

2) If there are any detected "wrong-Boolean-function" faults in A-CEG, correct these Boolean-functions for $\widehat{F}^B$.

3) If there are any virtual effects in $\widehat{E}^B$, add a new Boolean function for each of these virtual effects into $\widehat{E}^B$. These Boolean functions should always yield "0" for any input.

89

The process for determining $\widehat{CON}^B$ is:

1) Put all constraints of $\widehat{CON}^A$ into $\widehat{CON}^B$.

2) If there are any detected "introduction-of-an-undesired-constraint" faults in A-CEG, remove these extra constraints from $\widehat{CON}^B$.

3) If there are any detected "missing-a-constraint" faults in A-CEG, add appropriate constraints into $\widehat{CON}^B$.

In addition to the rules mentioned above, there are actions that should also be taken for A-CEG in case that an effect is missing to enable the automation of determining failure-relevant inputs. These actions are summarized in Table 5-1.

Table 5-1: Faults vs. Actions that should be taken for A-CEG or B-CEG

Fault in A-CEG	Actions taken for B-CEG	Actions taken for A-CEG
Omission of an effect	• Add a new effect identifier into $\hat{E}^B$. • Add an appropriate Boolean function into $\hat{F}^B$.	• Add an effect identifier (identical to its counterpart in B-CEG) into $\hat{E}^A$. This is a virtual effect in A-CEG. • Add a Boolean function into $\hat{F}^A$. This Boolean function should always yield "0" for any given input.
Introduction of an undesired effect	• Update the corresponding Boolean function in $\hat{F}^B$, such that it always yields "0" for any given input. This extra effect is a virtual effect in B-CEG and purposely left in B-CEG.	(None)

90

Fault in A-CEG	Actions taken for B-CEG	Actions taken for A-CEG
Omission of a constraint	• Adding an appropriate extra constraint into $\widehat{CON}^B$	(None)
Introduction of an undesired constraint	• Removing this extra constraint from $\widehat{CON}^B$	(None)
a wrong Boolean function- missing a cause	• Correct this Boolean function's expression for $\widehat{F}^B$ • If the cause is not in $\widehat{C}^B$, add a new cause identifier into $\widehat{C}^B$.	(None)
a wrong Boolean function- containing an extra cause	• Correct this Boolean function's expression for $\widehat{F}^B$ • If none of Boolean functions in $\widehat{F}^B$ contains this cause, remove this extra cause from $\widehat{C}^B$.	(None)
a wrong Boolean function- containing an incorrect logic operator	• Correct this Boolean function's expression for $\widehat{F}^B$	(None)

5.3.3 Introduction of Virtual Effect for Mating Missing or Extra Effects

Determination of the category of an input is achieved by pair-wisely mating all effects in A-CEG and B-CEG and pair-wisely comparing their outputs against the given input. However, there are two special cases in which there is an effect (of either A-CEG's or B-CEG's) that could not be mated:

Case 1: A-CEG is missing an effect. To rectify this fault, the missing effect should be added into B-CEG because B-CEG is the "faultless" version of

91

A-CEG. However, the newly added effect in B-CEG does not have any counterpart in A-CEG.

Case 2: A-CEG has an extra effect. To rectify this fault, the extra effect should be removed from B-CEG. However, this extra effect has to be kept in A-CEG because A-CEG should truly represent the faulty SRS. Thus the extra effect in A-CEG does not have any counterpart in B-CEG after the rectification action has been taken.

To handle these two special cases, the concept of the "*virtual effect*" is introduced. A *virtual effect* is an artifact added into A-CEG or B-CEG such that each effect in A-CEG and B-CEG has its counterpart. A virtual effect in A-CEG is corresponding to a missing-effect fault; a virtual effect in B-CEG is corresponding to an extra-effect fault. The use of virtual effects plays a key role in unifying the process of determining failure-relevant inputs (see Section 5.3.4 for details).

An example of adding virtual effects into CEG^A and CEG^B is illustrated in Figure 5-4. In this example, there are two assumed faults in A-CEG: a missing effect (e_2) and an extra effect (e_3).

According to Table 5-1, a virtual effect (e_2) is added into $\hat{E}^A$, and the corresponding Boolean function ($e_2 := 0$) is added into $\hat{F}^A$. Similarly, a virtual effect (e_3) is added into $\hat{E}^B$, and the corresponding Boolean function ($e_3 := 0$) is added into $\hat{F}^B$.

$$CEG^A \triangleq \left\{ \widehat{C}^A, \widehat{E}^A, \widehat{F}^A, \widehat{CON}^A \right\} \qquad CEG^B \triangleq \left\{ \widehat{C}^B, \widehat{E}^B, \widehat{F}^B, \widehat{CON}^B \right\}$$

$$\widehat{C}^A \triangleq \{c_1, c_2, c_3\} \qquad\qquad\qquad \widehat{C}^B \triangleq \{c_1, c_2, c_3\}$$

$$\widehat{E}^A \triangleq \{e_1, e_3, e_4\} \qquad\qquad\qquad \widehat{E}^B \triangleq \{e_1, e_2, e_4\}$$

$$\widehat{F}^A \triangleq \left\{ \begin{array}{l} e_1 := c_1; \\ e_3 := c_2 \cap c_3; \\ e_4 := c_3 \end{array} \right\} \qquad \widehat{F}^B \triangleq \left\{ \begin{array}{l} e_1 := c_1; \\ e_2 := c_1 \cup c_2; \\ e_4 := c_3 \end{array} \right\}$$

$$\widehat{CON}^A \triangleq \Phi \ (empty\ set) \qquad \widehat{CON}^B \triangleq \Phi \ (empty\ set)$$

a) before Adding Virtual Effects into A-CEG and B-CEG

$$CEG^A \triangleq \left\{ \widehat{C}^A, \widehat{E}^A, \widehat{F}^A, \widehat{CON}^A \right\} \qquad CEG^B \triangleq \left\{ \widehat{C}^B, \widehat{E}^B, \widehat{F}^B, \widehat{CON}^B \right\}$$

$$\widehat{C}^A \triangleq \{c_1, c_2, c_3\} \qquad\qquad\qquad \widehat{C}^B \triangleq \{c_1, c_2, c_3\}$$

$$\widehat{E}^A \triangleq \{e_1, e_2, e_3, e_4\} \qquad\qquad \widehat{E}^B \triangleq \{e_1, e_2, e_3, e_4\}$$

$$\widehat{F}^A \triangleq \left\{ \begin{array}{l} e_1 := c_1; \\ e_2 := 0; \\ e_3 := c_2 \cap c_3; \\ e_4 := c_3 \end{array} \right\} \qquad \widehat{F}^B \triangleq \left\{ \begin{array}{l} e_1 := c_1; \\ e_2 := c_1 \cup c_2; \\ e_3 := 0; \\ e_4 := c_3 \end{array} \right\}$$

$$\widehat{CON}^A \triangleq \Phi \ (empty\ set) \qquad \widehat{CON}^B \triangleq \Phi \ (empty\ set)$$

b) after Adding Virtual Effects into A-CEG and B-CEG

Figure 5-4: Example of Adding Virtual Effects into A-CEG and B-CEG

5.3.4 Determination of an Effect's Output

When determining the response (output) of a regular (neither missing nor extra) effect, constraints have higher precedence than the corresponding Boolean function. If any constraint is applicable to the effect (in case of "MASK" constraint) or to the given input (in case of "REQUIRE", "INCLUSIVE", "EXCLUSIVE", or "ONE-ONLY-ONE" constraint), the effect should yield "NA" (short for "Not Allowed");

otherwise, the effect's response should be determined by its Boolean function, taking a value of either "0" or "1".

The constraint lemmas (Lemma 3-1 to Lemma 3-6) are very helpful when determining if a constraint is applicable to an effect or a given output or not. The violation of any of these lemmas caused by a constraint indicates the applicability of the constraint to the effect and/or the given input.

Apparently, a *virtual effect* should not be triggered under any circumstance because it is not a physical entity. Therefore, the Boolean function corresponding to a virtual effect should always yield "0" for any given input, unless any constraint is applicable to the given input (in this case, "NA" is assigned as the output for the virtual effect). In contrast with a non-virtual effect, which can take a value of "0", "1", or "NA", a virtual effect can only take a value of either "0" or "NA". Thus, we have the following two lemmas in regard to determining the output for a virtual effect:

Lemma 5-2: Missing Effect's Output

If e_j^A is a virtual effect in $\hat{E}^A$,

$$f_j^A\left(\overline{X}\right) \equiv 0, \text{ and}$$

$$e_j^A\left(\overline{X}\right) = \begin{cases} NA & \text{if any constraint in } \widehat{CON}^A \text{ is applicable;} \\ 0 & \text{otherwise.} \end{cases}$$

where $\overline{X}$ is any given input.

Lemma 5-3: Extra Effect's Output

94

If e_j^B is a virtual effect in $\hat{E}^B$,

$$f_j^B\left(\overline{X}\right) \equiv 0, \text{ and}$$

$$e_j^B\left(\overline{X}\right) = \begin{cases} NA & \text{if any constraint in } \widehat{CON}^B \text{ is applicable;} \\ 0 & \text{otherwise.} \end{cases}$$

where $\overline{X}$ is any given input.

With the help of Lemma 5-2 and Lemma 5-3, the process of determining the output of an effect (of either A-CEG's or B-CEG) against a given input can be unified, as depicted in Figure 5-5.

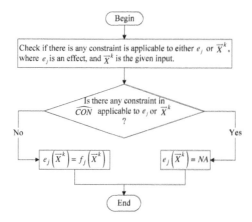

Figure 5-5: Unified Process for Determining the Output of an Effect

5.3.5 Algorithm for Determining the Category of an Input

An input falls into the category of either failure-relevant or failure-irrelevant. To determine the category of an input, outputs of all effects in A-CEG and B-CEG are

95

pair-wisely compared. If there is one (or more) effect pair(s) that yields different output, the input is failure-relevant; otherwise, it is failure-irrelevant. The detailed algorithm for determining the category of an input is shown in Figure 5-6.

Usually it does not matter in which sequence the effect pairs are chosen to examine the category of a given input. One convenient way is to select effect pairs by the ascending/descending order of the effect identifiers' subscript. However, in case of the presence of any "MASK" constraint(s) in $\overline{CON}^A$ or $\overline{CON}^B$, the output of "Masker" effect must be determined before the output of the "Maskee" effect can be determined. Otherwise, there is no way to correctly judge if a "MASK" constraint is applicable for a "Maskee" effect or not. For instance, in case of $MASK(e_1, e_2)$ (e_1 masking e_2), e_1 is a "Masker" effect and e_2 is a "Maskee" effect. The output for e_1 should be determined before determining that of e_2's. For this case, the selection precedence of e_1 pair is higher than that of the e_2 pair's.

It should be noted that the algorithm shown in Figure 5-6 is ready for automation since there are many techniques and automation tools [77][78] available for evaluation of Boolean logic formula. These techniques and tools are shown to have excellent scalability when being applied to VLSI (Very Large Scale Integrated logical circuits) design and test, where there are usually millions of variables (a variable in VLSI design and test is equivalent to a cause in this study). It is unlikely that an SRS will contain millions of causes, even for a very large-scale system, such as Windows Vista®. Therefore, we believe that there should be no scalability issue in determining the failure-relevant inputs if we have developed tools based on the algorithm shown in Figure 5-6 and taking advantages of the existing tools for Boolean logic formula reduction.

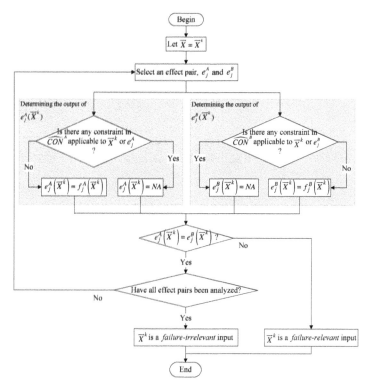

Figure 5-6: Algorithm for Determining the Category of a Given Input $\overline{X}^k$

5.3.6 Examples of Identifying Failure-relevant Inputs

In this section, we use a sample A-CEG (shown in Figure 5-7) to illustrate how to identify failure-relevant inputs for the seven basic types of A-CEG faults (see Section

97

4.5.1 for definitions of the A-CEG fault categories). For the sake of simplicity and without loss of generality, assume that there is only one type of faults in each case.

$$CEG^A \triangleq \left\{ \widehat{C}^A, \widehat{E}^A, \widehat{F}^A, \widehat{CON}^A \right\}$$

$$\widehat{C}^A \triangleq \{c_1, c_2, c_3\}$$

$$\widehat{E}^A \triangleq \{e_1, e_2\}$$

$$\widehat{F}^A \triangleq \left\{ \begin{array}{l} e_1 := c_1; \\ e_2 := c_1 \cup (c_2 \cap c_3) \end{array} \right\}$$

$$\widehat{CON}^A \triangleq \{REQUIRE(c_1, c_2)\}$$

Figure 5-7: Mathematical Expression of the Sample A-CEG

5.3.6.1. Case 1: A-CEG is missing an effect

Assume that e_3 is the missing effect and its Boolean function is $e_3 := c_3$.

According to Table 5-1, e_3 and its Boolean function $e_3 := c_3$ are added into B-CEG. Besides, a virtual effect with identity e_3 is added into A-CEG, and $e_3 := 0$ is assigned as its Boolean function. The revised A-CEG and B-CEG for this case is illustrated in Figure 5-8.

$$CEG^A \triangleq \left\{ \widehat{C}^A, \widehat{E}^A, \widehat{F}^A, \widehat{CON}^A \right\} \qquad CEG^B \triangleq \left\{ \widehat{C}^B, \widehat{E}^B, \widehat{F}^B, \widehat{CON}^B \right\}$$

$$\widehat{C}^A \triangleq \{c_1, c_2, c_3\} \qquad\qquad \widehat{C}^B \triangleq \{c_1, c_2, c_3\}$$

$$\widehat{E}^A \triangleq \{e_1, e_2, e_3\} \qquad\qquad \widehat{E}^B \triangleq \{e_1, e_2, e_3\}$$

$$\widehat{F}^A \triangleq \left\{ \begin{array}{l} e_1 := c_1; \\ e_2 := c_1 \cup (c_2 \cap c_3); \\ e_3 := 0 \end{array} \right\} \qquad \widehat{F}^B \triangleq \left\{ \begin{array}{l} e_1 := c_1; \\ e_2 := c_1 \cup (c_2 \cap c_3); \\ e_3 := c_3 \end{array} \right\}$$

$$\widehat{CON}^A \triangleq \{REQUIRE(c_1, c_2)\} \qquad \widehat{CON}^B \triangleq \{REQUIRE(c_1, c_2)\}$$

Figure 5-8: Revised A-CEG and B-CEG for Case 1

By applying the unified effect output determination process shown in Figure 5-5,
we determined and summarized all effects' outputs for this case, as shown in Table 5-
2. In this table, the output that is in disagreement with its counterpart is highlighted
with a shadow box.

Apparently, the failure-relevant inputs for this case are $\bar{c}_1 \cap \bar{c}_2 \cap c_3$ ($k = 2$), and
$\bar{c}_1 \cap c_2 \cap c_3$ ($k = 4$).

Table 5-2: Effects' Outputs for Case 1

index, k	Input $\vec{X}^k$			e_1		e_2		e_3	
	c_1	c_2	c_3	of A-CEG's	of B-CEG's	of A-CEG's	of B-CEG's	of A-CEG's	of B-CEG's
1	0	0	0	0	0	0	0	0	0
2	0	0	1	0	0	0	0	0	1
3	0	1	0	0	0	0	0	0	0
4	0	1	1	0	0	1	1	0	1
5	1	0	0	NA	NA	NA	NA	NA	NA
6	1	0	1	NA	NA	NA	NA	NA	NA
7	1	1	0	1	1	1	1	0	0
8	1	1	1	1	1	1	1	0	1

5.3.6.2. Case 2: A-CEG has an extra effect

Assume e_1 is the extra effect.

According to Table 5-1, a virtual effect with identity e_1 is added into B-CEG and
$e_1 := 0$ is assigned as its Boolean function. The A-CEG and B-CEG for this case is
illustrated in Figure 5-9.

$$CEG^A \triangleq \left\{ \hat{C}^A, \hat{E}^A, \hat{F}^A, \widehat{CON}^A \right\} \qquad CEG^B \triangleq \left\{ \hat{C}^B, \hat{E}^B, \hat{F}^B, \widehat{CON}^B \right\}$$

$$\hat{C}^A \triangleq \{c_1, c_2, c_3\} \qquad\qquad\qquad \hat{C}^B \triangleq \{c_1, c_2, c_3\}$$

$$\hat{E}^A \triangleq \{e_1, e_2\} \qquad\qquad\qquad\quad \hat{E}^B \triangleq \{e_1, e_2\}$$

$$\hat{F}^A \triangleq \left\{ \begin{array}{l} e_1 := c_1; \\ e_2 := c_1 \cup (c_2 \cap c_3) \end{array} \right\} \qquad \hat{F}^B \triangleq \left\{ \begin{array}{l} e_1 := 0; \\ e_2 := c_1 \cup (c_2 \cap c_3) \end{array} \right\}$$

$$\widehat{CON}^A \triangleq \{REQUIRE(c_1, c_2)\} \qquad \widehat{CON}^B \triangleq \{REQUIRE(c_1, c_2)\}$$

Figure 5-9: Revised A-CEG and B-CEG for Case 2

By employing the unified effect output determination process shown in Figure 5-5, we determined and summarized all effects' outputs for this case, as shown in Table 5-3. In this table, the output that is in disagreement with its counterpart is highlighted with a shadow box.

Apparently, the failure-relevant inputs for this case are $c_1 \cap c_2 \cap \bar{c}_3$ ($k = 7$) and $c_1 \cap c_2 \cap c_3$ ($k = 8$).

Table 5-3: Effects' Outputs for Case 2

index, k	Input $\vec{X}^k$			e_1		e_2	
	c_1	c_2	c_3	of A-CEG's	of B-CEG's	of A-CEG's	of B-CEG's
1	0	0	0	0	0	0	0
2	0	0	1	0	0	0	0
3	0	1	0	0	0	0	0
4	0	1	1	0	0	1	1
5	1	0	0	NA	NA	NA	NA
6	1	0	1	NA	NA	NA	NA
7	1	1	0	1	0	1	1
8	1	1	1	1	0	1	1

Assume $MASK(e_1, e_2)$ is the missing constraint.

According to Table 5-1, $MASK(e_1, e_2)$ is added into B-CEG. The A-CEG and B-CEG for this case is illustrated in Figure 5-10.

$$CEG^A \triangleq \left\{ \hat{C}^A, \hat{E}^A, \hat{F}^A, \widehat{CON}^A \right\} \qquad CEG^B \triangleq \left\{ \hat{C}^B, \hat{E}^B, \hat{F}^B, \widehat{CON}^B \right\}$$

$$\hat{C}^A \triangleq \{c_1, c_2, c_3\} \qquad\qquad \hat{C}^B \triangleq \{c_1, c_2, c_3\}$$

$$\hat{E}^A \triangleq \{e_1, e_2\} \qquad\qquad \hat{E}^B \triangleq \{e_1, e_2\}$$

$$\hat{F}^A \triangleq \left\{ \begin{matrix} e_1 := c_1; \\ e_2 := c_1 \cup (c_2 \cap c_3) \end{matrix} \right\} \qquad \hat{F}^B \triangleq \left\{ \begin{matrix} e_1 := c_1; \\ e_2 := c_1 \cup (c_2 \cap c_3) \end{matrix} \right\}$$

$$\widehat{CON}^A \triangleq \{REQUIRE(c_1, c_2)\} \qquad \widehat{CON}^B \triangleq \left\{ \begin{matrix} REQUIRE(c_1, c_2); \\ MASK(e_1, e_2) \end{matrix} \right\}$$

Figure 5-10: Revised A-CEG and B-CEG for Case 3

By employing the unified effect output determination process shown in Figure 5-5, we determined and summarized all effects' outputs for this case, as shown in Table 5-4. In this table, the output that is in disagreement with its counterpart is highlighted with a shadow box.

Apparently, the failure-relevant inputs for this case are $c_1 \cap c_2 \cap \bar{c}_3$ ($k = 7$) and $c_1 \cap c_2 \cap c_3$ ($k = 8$).

Table 5-4: Effects' Outputs for Case 3

index, k	Input $\vec{X}^k$			e_1		e_2	
	c_1	c_2	c_3	of A-CEG's	of B-CEG's	of A-CEG's	of B-CEG's
1	0	0	0	0	0	0	0

index, k	Input $\vec{X}^k$			e_1		e_2	
	c_1	c_2	c_3	of A-CEG's	of B-CEG's	of A-CEG's	of B-CEG's
2	0	0	1	0	0	0	0
3	0	1	0	0	0	0	0
4	0	1	1	0	0	1	1
5	1	0	0	NA	NA	NA	NA
6	1	0	1	NA	NA	NA	NA
7	1	1	0	1	1	1	NA
8	1	1	1	1	1	1	NA

5.3.6.4. Case 4: A-CEG has an extra constraint

Assume $REQUIRE(c_1, c_2)$ is the extra constraint.

According to Table 5-1, $REQUIRE(c_1, c_2)$ is removed from B-CEG. The A-CEG and B-CEG for this case is illustrated in Figure 5-11.

$$CEG^A \triangleq \left\{ \widehat{C}^A, \widehat{E}^A, \widehat{F}^A, \widehat{CON}^A \right\} \qquad CEG^B \triangleq \left\{ \widehat{C}^B, \widehat{E}^B, \widehat{F}^B, \widehat{CON}^B \right\}$$

$$\widehat{C}^A \triangleq \{c_1, c_2, c_3\} \qquad \widehat{C}^B \triangleq \{c_1, c_2, c_3\}$$

$$\widehat{E}^A \triangleq \{e_1, e_2\} \qquad \widehat{E}^B \triangleq \{e_1, e_2\}$$

$$\widehat{F}^A \triangleq \left\{ \begin{matrix} e_1 := c_1; \\ e_2 := c_1 \cup (c_2 \cap c_3) \end{matrix} \right\} \qquad \widehat{F}^B \triangleq \left\{ \begin{matrix} e_1 := c_1; \\ e_2 := c_1 \cup (c_2 \cap c_3) \end{matrix} \right\}$$

$$\widehat{CON}^A \triangleq \{REQUIRE(c_1, c_2)\} \qquad \widehat{CON}^B \triangleq \Phi(\text{empty set})$$

Figure 5-11: Revised A-CEG and B-CEG for Case 4

By employing the unified effect output determination process shown in Figure 5-5, we determined and summarized all effects' outputs for this case, as shown in Table 5-5. In this table, the output that is in disagreement with its counterpart is highlighted with a shadow box.

Apparently, the failure-relevant inputs for this case are $c_1 \cap \bar{c}_2 \cap \bar{c}_3$ ($k = 5$) and $c_1 \cap \bar{c}_2 \cap c_3$ ($k = 6$).

Table 5-5: Effects' Outputs for Case 4

index, k	Input $\vec{X}^k$			e_1		e_2	
	c_1	c_2	c_3	of A-CEG's	of B-CEG's	of A-CEG's	of B-CEG's
1	0	0	0	0	0	0	0
2	0	0	1	0	0	0	0
3	0	1	0	0	0	0	0
4	0	1	1	0	0	1	1
5	1	0	0	NA	1	NA	1
6	1	0	1	NA	1	NA	1
7	1	1	0	1	1	1	1
8	1	1	1	1	1	1	1

5.3.6.5. Case 5: A-CEG has a wrong Boolean function that is missing a cause

Assume the desired Boolean function for effect e_1 is $e_1 := c_1 \cup c_4$ rather than $e_1 := c_1$ (c_4 is the missing cause).

According to Table 5-1, the desired Boolean function for e_1 is updated in B-CEG. The A-CEG and B-CEG for this case is illustrated in Figure 5-12.

$$CEG^A \triangleq \left\{ \hat{C}^A, \hat{E}^A, \hat{F}^A, \widehat{CON}^A \right\} \qquad CEG^B \triangleq \left\{ \hat{C}^B, \hat{E}^B, \hat{F}^B, \widehat{CON}^B \right\}$$

$$\hat{C}^A \triangleq \{c_1, c_2, c_3\} \qquad \hat{C}^B \triangleq \{c_1, c_2, c_3, c_4\}$$

$$\hat{E}^A \triangleq \{e_1, e_2\} \qquad \hat{E}^B \triangleq \{e_1, e_2\}$$

$$\hat{F}^A \triangleq \left\{ \begin{matrix} e_1 := c_1; \\ e_2 := c_1 \cup (c_2 \cap c_3) \end{matrix} \right\} \qquad \hat{F}^B \triangleq \left\{ \begin{matrix} e_1 := c_1 \cup c_4; \\ e_2 := c_1 \cup (c_2 \cap c_3) \end{matrix} \right\}$$

$$\widehat{CON}^A \triangleq \{REQUIRE(c_1, c_2)\} \qquad \widehat{CON}^B \triangleq \{REQUIRE(c_1, c_2)\}$$

Figure 5-12: Revised A-CEG and B-CEG for Case 5

By employing the unified effect output determination process shown in Figure 5-5, we determined and summarized all effects' outputs for this case, as shown in Table 5-6. In this table, the output that is in disagreement with its counterpart is highlighted with a shadow box.

Apparently, the failure-relevant inputs for this case are $\bar{c}_1 \cap \bar{c}_2 \cap \bar{c}_3 \cap c_4$ ($k = 2$),

$\bar{c}_1 \cap \bar{c}_2 \cap c_3 \cap c_4$ ($k = 4$), $\bar{c}_1 \cap c_2 \cap \bar{c}_3 \cap c_4$ ($k = 6$), and $\bar{c}_1 \cap c_2 \cap c_3 \cap c_4$ ($k = 8$).

Table 5-6: Effects' Outputs for Case 5

index, k	Input $\vec{X}^k$				e_1		e_2	
	c_1	c_2	c_3	c_4	of A-CEG's	of B-CEG's	of A-CEG's	of B-CEG's
1	0	0	0	0	0	0	0	0
2	0	0	0	1	0	1	0	0
3	0	0	1	0	0	0	0	0
4	0	0	1	1	0	1	1	1
5	0	1	0	0	0	0	0	0
6	0	1	0	1	0	1	0	0
7	0	1	1	0	0	0	0	0
8	0	1	1	1	0	1	1	1
9	1	0	0	0	NA	NA	NA	NA
10	1	0	0	1	NA	NA	NA	NA
11	1	0	1	0	NA	NA	NA	NA
12	1	0	1	1	NA	NA	NA	NA
13	1	1	0	0	1	1	1	1
14	1	1	0	1	1	1	1	1
15	1	1	1	0	1	1	1	1
16	1	1	1	1	1	1	1	1

Assume the desired Boolean function for effect e_2 is $e_2 := c_2 \cap c_3$ rather than

$e_2 := c_1 \cup (c_2 \cap c_3)$ (c_1 is an extra cause).

According to Table 5-1, the desired Boolean function for effect e_2 is updated in B-CEG. The revised A-CEG and B-CEG for this case is illustrated in Figure 5-13.

$$CEG^A \triangleq \left\{ \widehat{C}^A, \widehat{E}^A, \widehat{F}^A, \widehat{CON}^A \right\} \qquad CEG^B \triangleq \left\{ \widehat{C}^B, \widehat{E}^B, \widehat{F}^B, \widehat{CON}^B \right\}$$

$$\widehat{C}^A \triangleq \{c_1, c_2, c_3\} \qquad\qquad \widehat{C}^B \triangleq \{c_1, c_2, c_3\}$$

$$\widehat{E}^A \triangleq \{e_1, e_2\} \qquad\qquad \widehat{E}^B \triangleq \{e_1, e_2\}$$

$$\widehat{F}^A \triangleq \left\{ \begin{array}{l} e_1 := c_1; \\ e_2 := c_1 \cup (c_2 \cap c_3) \end{array} \right\} \qquad \widehat{F}^B \triangleq \left\{ \begin{array}{l} e_1 := c_1; \\ e_2 := c_2 \cap c_3 \end{array} \right\}$$

$$\widehat{CON}^A \triangleq \{REQUIRE(c_1, c_2)\} \qquad \widehat{CON}^B \triangleq \{REQUIRE(c_1, c_2)\}$$

Figure 5-13: Revised A-CEG and B-CEG for Case 6

By employing the unified effect output determination process shown in Figure 5-5, we determined and summarized all effects' outputs for this case, as shown in Table 5-7. In this table, the output that is in disagreement with its counterpart is highlighted with a shadow box.

Apparently, the only failure-relevant input for this case is $c_1 \cap c_2 \cap \bar{c}_3$ ($k = 7$).

Table 5-7: Effects' Outputs for Case 6

index, k	Input $\vec{X}^k$			e_1		e_2	
	c_1	c_2	c_3	of A-CEG's	of B-CEG's	of A-CEG's	of B-CEG's
1	0	0	0	0	0	0	0
2	0	0	1	0	0	0	0

3	0	1	0	0	0	0	0
4	0	1	1	0	0	1	1
5	1	0	0	NA	NA	NA	NA
6	1	0	1	NA	NA	NA	NA
7	1	1	0	1	1	1	0
8	1	1	1	1	1	1	1

5.3.6.7. Case 7: A-CEG has a wrong Boolean function which contains incorrect logic operators

Assume the desired Boolean function for effect e_2 is $e_2 := c_1 \cap (c_2 \cup c_3)$ rather than $e_2 := c_1 \cup (c_2 \cap c_3)$.

According to Table 5-1, the desired Boolean function for effect e_2 is updated in B-CEG. The A-CEG and B-CEG for this case is illustrated in Figure 5-14.

$$CEG^A \triangleq \left\{ \hat{C}^A, \hat{E}^A, \hat{F}^A, \widehat{CON}^A \right\} \qquad CEG^B \triangleq \left\{ \hat{C}^B, \hat{E}^B, \hat{F}^B, \widehat{CON}^B \right\}$$

$$\hat{C}^A \triangleq \{c_1, c_2, c_3\} \qquad\qquad \hat{C}^B \triangleq \{c_1, c_2, c_3\}$$

$$\hat{E}^A \triangleq \{e_1, e_2\} \qquad\qquad \hat{E}^B \triangleq \{e_1, e_2\}$$

$$\hat{F}^A \triangleq \left\{ \begin{matrix} e_1 := c_1; \\ e_2 := c_1 \cup (c_2 \cap c_3) \end{matrix} \right\} \qquad \hat{F}^B \triangleq \left\{ \begin{matrix} e_1 := c_1; \\ e_2 := c_1 \cap (c_2 \cup c_3) \end{matrix} \right\}$$

$$\widehat{CON}^A \triangleq \{REQUIRE(c_1, c_2)\} \qquad \widehat{CON}^B \triangleq \{REQUIRE(c_1, c_2)\}$$

Figure 5-14: Revised A-CEG and B-CEG for Case 7

By employing the unified effect output determination process shown in Figure 5-5, we determined and summarized all effects' outputs for this case, as shown in Table 5-8. In this table, the output that is in disagreement with its counterpart is highlighted with a shadow box.

Apparently, the only failure-relevant input for this case is $\bar{c}_1 \cap c_2 \cap c_3$ $(k = 4)$.

Table 5-8: Effects' Outputs for Case 7

index, k	Input $\vec{X}^k$			e_1		e_2	
	c_1	c_2	c_3	of A-CEG's	of B-CEG's	of A-CEG's	of B-CEG's
1	0	0	0	0	0	0	0
2	0	0	1	0	0	0	0
3	0	1	0	0	0	0	0
4	0	1	1	0	0	1	0
5	1	0	0	NA	NA	NA	NA
6	1	0	1	NA	NA	NA	NA
7	1	1	0	1	1	1	1
8	1	1	1	1	1	1	1

5.4 *Calculation of the Occurrence Probability of Failure-relevant Inputs*

According to Lemma 5-1, the event "An A-CEG fails" is equivalent to the union of identified failure-relevant inputs. Therefore, this event can be expressed in the form of a fault tree, as depicted in Figure 5-15.

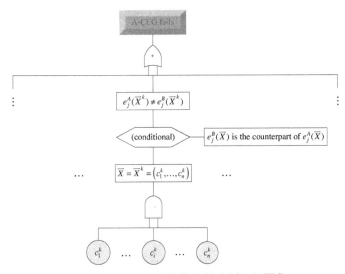

Figure 5-15: Generic Fault Tree Model for A-CEG

Thus the task of calculating the occurrence probability of the event "an A-CEG fails" can be decomposed into two sub-tasks:

Sub-task 1: Constructing a fault tree representing the union of all failure-relevant inputs.

Sub-task 2: Calculating the occurrence probability of the top event of the fault tree.

Binary Decision Diagram (BDD) techniques are widely used for fault tree analysis. With the help of BDD techniques, the task of calculating the occurrence probability of the event "an A-CEG fails" is achieved by accomplishing the following two sub-tasks:

Sub-task 1: Constructing a BDD for the fault tree representing the union of all

108

failure-relevant inputs;

Sub-task 2: Calculating the probability of the BDD's top node.

5.4.1 Representation of a Boolean Expression Using BDD Techniques

The use of Binary Decision Diagrams as a representation of Boolean expressions is regarded the most powerful approach for fault tree analysis [79] [80]. The BDD method does not analyze the fault tree directly, but converts the tree to a binary decision diagram, which represents the Boolean equation for the top event [80].

A *Binary Decision Diagram* (BDD) is a data structure that is used to represent a Boolean function. A Boolean function can be represented as a rooted, directed, acyclic graph, which consists of decision nodes and two terminal nodes called 0-terminal and 1-terminal. Each decision node is labeled by a Boolean variable and has two child nodes called low child and high child. The edge from a node to a low (high) child represents an assignment of the variable to 0 (1). Such a BDD is called 'ordered' if different variables appear in the same order on all paths from the root. It is called 'reduced' if the graph is reduced according to two rules [81]:

• Merge any isomorphic sub-graphs.

• Eliminate any node whose two children are isomorphic.

In popular usage, the term BDD almost always refers to *Reduced Ordered Binary Decision Diagram* (ROBDD) in the literature. The advantage of an ROBDD is that it is canonical (unique) for a particular functionality. This property makes it useful in functional equivalence checking and other operations like functional technology mapping. Figure 5-16 shows an example of a BDD for the Boolean function

109

$f = xy + z$.

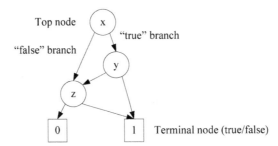

Figure 5-16: Example of BDD for the Boolean Function $f = xy + z$

BDD-based algorithms offer advantages in terms of accuracy and efficiency [80]:

- Efficient manipulation of logic.

- Straightforward treatment of incoherent logic.

- Exact quantification': no need to use rare-event type approximations.

- Graphical representation of Boolean Expressions.

There are several BDD generation software packages for free, such as CUDD (by Colorado University), CAL (by UC Berkeley), and BuDDy (by IT-University of Copenhagen). This study uses the BuDDy package [82] to convert the Boolean expression of the union of all failure-relevant inputs into a BDD.

BuDDy is a powerful library for Boolean expression manipulation; it combines as easily as a C++ interface and is an efficient implementation based on the novel BDD data structure. Although one can work with BuDDy without understanding what BDDs are, it is worth understanding the concept of BDD structure and usage when developing large applications that are heavily based on Boolean expression. An

110

example of using the BuDDy package to construct a BDD for the Boolean logic of "an A-CEG Fails" is given in Appendix B.

5.4.2 Recursive Algorithm for Calculating the Occurrence Probability of a BDD's Top Node

After the BDD that represents the Boolean logic of the union of failure-relevant inputs is constructed, the recursive algorithm shown in Figure 5-17 can be used to calculate the probability of a BDD's top node. This recursive algorithm is derived from [80][26].

The operational profile (see Section 5.4.3) is required to do the calculation, and only the operational profile for causes that appears in failure-relevant inputs is needed.

We developed a tool to calculate the occurrence probability of a BDD's top node. This tool is based on the BuDDy package [82] and the recursive algorithm shown in Figure 5-17. The sample source code of using this tool is illustrated in Appendix B.

```
Bdd_Prob_Cal(X)
/* X = ite (xᵢ, T, F),
  T = "True" branch of node xi
  F = "False" branch of node xi
  P_T = Probability of "True" branch reach terminal node "1"
  P_F = Probability of "False" branch reach terminal node "1"
*/
{
    /*Consider "True" branch*/
    If T is terminal node "1"
        P_T = 1.0
    else if T is terminal node "0"
        P_T = 0.0
    else
    /*Go deeper to find the probability of T by recursively calling this function*/
        P_T = Bdd_Prob_Cal (T)
    /*Consider "False" branch*/
    If F is terminal node "1"
        P_F = 1.0
    else if F is terminal node "0"
        P_F = 0.0
    else
    /*Go deeper to find the probability of F by recursively calling this function*/
        P_F = Bdd_Prob_Cal (F)

    Probability[X] = Probability[xᵢ] × P_T + (1- Probability[xᵢ]) × P_F
    Return (Probability[X])
}
```

Figure 5-17: Recursive Algorithm for Calculating the Occurrence Probability of a
BDD's Top Node

5.4.3 Operational Profile (OP)

It is obvious that the usage of the software is a very important constituent element in software reliability quantification. Therefore, the expected usage must be taken into consideration when estimating/predicting software reliability [3].

There exist several techniques to specify the usage, including Operational Profile (OP), and Markov usage model etc [83]. These techniques are different approaches to model the software usage in order to specify the same.

An *operational profile* (OP) is the estimated relative frequency for each "operation" that a system under test supports [84]. It associates a set of probabilities to the program input space and therefore describes the behavior of the system [84].

OP is traditionally evaluated by enumerating field inputs and evaluating their occurrence frequencies. Musa [84] pioneered a five-step approach to develop OP. His approach is based on collecting information on customers and users, identifying the system modes, determining the functional profile, and recording the input states and their associated occurrence probabilities experienced in field operation.

Musa's approach has been widely utilized and adapted in the literature to generate OP [85]. For instance, Elbaum and Narla [86] refined Musa's approach by addressing heterogeneous user groups. They discovered that a single operational profile only "averages" the usage and "obscures" the real information about the operational probabilities. They utilized clustering to identify groups of similar customers. Sandfoss [85] suggests that estimation of occurrence probabilities could be based on numbers obtained from project documentation, engineering judgment, and system development experience. Gittens et al [87] proposed an extended OP model which is

113

composed of the process profile, structural profile, and data profile. The process profile addresses the processes and associated frequencies. The structural profile accounts for the system structure, the configuration or structure of the actual application, and the data profile covers the inputs to the application from different users.

Musa's approach and other extended approaches all use an assumption that field data or historic usage data cover the entire input domain. This assumption is not always true and their approaches are not always successful simply because some input data may not be available, especially for safety critical control systems [40].

Addressing to this issue, the UMD research team [40] extended these approaches and generated a systematic method to identify those environmental variables and estimate all the environmental inputs.

Generating OP at earlier development phases is even more challenging. However, instead of discussing this open topic, this study assumes that the associated OP has already been collected before using the algorithm shown in Figure 5-1 to predict reliability for a software system. Moreover, it is assumed that OP is given in the form of a set of occurrence probabilities for all distinct causes that appear in the failure-relevant inputs.

5.5 Summary

This chapter presents an automation-oriented algorithm for quantifying the impact of detected faults on software reliability applicable in requirements analysis stage. The proposed quantification algorithm is also applicable during later development phases, such as coding and testing phase, where the potential savings are less.

Chapter 6: Examination of the Applicability of the Proposed CEGA Techniques for Early-stage Software Reliability Prediction by Case Studies

A rigorous definition of software measurement does not guarantee its applicability (in terms of feasibility and scalability) in practice.

Feasibility is an indispensable attribute of a technique, which indicates its capability of being used or dealt with successfully.

Scalability is a desirable attribute of a technique, which indicates its ability to either handle growing amounts of work in a graceful manner, or to be readily enlarged. One serious drawback of past and current software engineering research is lack of scalability. Researchers have developed techniques that work only on small systems. Mathematical techniques have, for the most part, been used only on very limited properties and on unrealistically small problems. Most any analysis technique works on a toy problem. There is reason to believe that software development in the large is so different than the toy problems found in most research papers that many published techniques may not apply to real projects. We need to find a balance of formal and informal techniques that scale by considering problems of realistic size and complexity from the start. Given the complexity of the systems we are attempting to build, the only convincing argument that an approach will work in practice is to validate techniques on real systems.

To evaluate the feasibility and scalability of the proposed CEGA techniques for quantification of software reliability at an early development stage, we conducted two case studies. The first case study was carried out against a smaller application, whose SRS has 32 pages and 402 sentences[4]. The second case study was against a larger application, whose SRS has 289 pages and 3492 sentences.

This chapter reports the procedure, results and analysis of these two case studies.

6.1 Applications Used Case Studies

The smaller application used in the first case study is *Personal Access Control System (PACS)* [88]. PACS is a simplified version of an automated personnel entry access system used to provide privileged physical access to rooms/buildings. PACS system provides physical access to a restricted area to authorized users based on a personal ID card and personal identification number (PIN). In order to get access, the user swipes an ID card which contains user's name and social security number (SSN) through a card reader. After using its database of user's names and SSNs to validate user's privileges, PACS system instructs the user to enter a four-digit PIN number. If the entered PIN matches a stored PIN, the system allows the user to enter the area through a gate. PACS guides the user of the system with messages written on a single-line display screen. A security officer monitors and controls the PACS using a console with another single-line display screen, an alarm, a reset button, and a gate

---

[4] Note that the numbers of sentences measured in this study were all rough estimates because we did not adopt any strict rules for sentence counting.

override button. In its current form, requirements specification for PACS originated from a US government agency.

The larger application used in the second case study is called "*SXXX*", because this application is copyrighted and its real name is not allowed to be exposed to the public. SXXX [40] is a safety-critical and real-time software system used in the nuclear domain. The SXXX System is based on the SXXX Processor Module. The SXXX Processor Module contains both discrete and high level analog input and output circuits. These circuits read input signals from the plant and send outputs that can be used to provide trips or actuations of safety system equipment, control a process, or provide alarms and indications. The transfer functions performed between the inputs and outputs are dependent on the software that is installed in the module. The SXXX system was installed in 1995 to partially upgrade an existing analog reactor protection system.

6.2 *Procedure*

The two case studies are called Case Study A and Case Study B.

Case Study A: Applying the proposed CEGA techniques to PACS. The primary purpose of this case study is to examine the feasibility of the proposed techniques.

Case Study B: Applying the proposed CEGA techniques to SXXX. The primary purpose of this case study is to examine the scalability of the proposed techniques.

We hired a graduate student to carry out these two case studies. Case Study A was conducted first. After the feasibility of the proposed techniques was confirmed in Case Study A, Case Study B was conducted to examine the scalability of the proposed techniques. Administrative measures were taken to ensure the quality of results, such as partially validating the results by the author.

The same steps were taken for both case studies. These steps are as follows:

Step 1: Construct an A-CEG for the SRS and document any detected faults. The A-CEG is expressed in the mathematical format.

Step 2: Detect faults in the SRS.

Step 3: Quantify the impact of detected faults on software reliability.

Step 4: Document all results.

The techniques and tools required to perform these steps are summarized in Table 6-1.

Table 6-1: Steps vs. Required Techniques/Tools[*]

Steps	Task	Sub task	Required techniques/tools
Step 1	A-CEG construction	Identifying causes	• The general CEG construction procedure and the general CEG construction guidelines (described in Section 3.2)
		Identifying effects	

---

[*] In this table, the "General CEG construction procedure and the general CEG construction guidelines", "CEGA-based ambiguities review list", and "BDD techniques" were developed by others rather than the author.

118

Steps	Task	Sub task	Required techniques/tools
		Identifying logical relationships	• Mathematical expression of CEG (described in Section 3.5)
		Identifying constraints	
Step 2	Detection of SRS faults	Detecting SRS ambiguities	• CEGA-based ambiguities review list (described in Section 4.5.2)
		Validating A-CEG	• CEG validating technique (described in Section 4.5.3)
Step 3	Quantification of the impact of detected faults on software reliability	A-CEG revision	• A-CEG revision and B-A-CEG Construction Rules (described in Section 5.3.2)
		B-CEG construction	
		Identifying failure-relevant inputs	• Failure-relevant identification algorithm (described in Section 5.3)
		BDD construction	• BDD techniques for fault tree expression (described in Section 5.4.1) • the BuDDy package [82]
		Calculating the occurrence probability of BDD's top node	• The Fundamental Lemma (Lemma 5-1) • Recursive algorithm (shown in Figure 5-17) • BDD top node occurrence probability calculation tool. The sample source code of using this tool is illustrated in Appendix B.
Step 5	Documentation of results	(None)	(None)

6.3 Results and Findings

Both case studies (Case Study A and Case Study B) clearly confirmed the technical feasibility of the proposed techniques for software reliability prediction at an early development stage.

Table 6-2 summarizes the tasks, the required techniques to perform the tasks, and the scalability of the techniques in these two experiments.

119

Table 6-2: Scalability of the Proposed Techniques[*]

Task	Sub task	Proposed techniques	Comments on the scalability
A-CEG construction	Identifying causes	• General A-CEG construction guidelines • Mathematical expression of CEG	Scalability of using Mathematical expressions for A-CEG was confirmed. Scalability of identifying A-CEG elements (causes, effects, logical relationships, and constraints) using the general guidelines was not scalable.
	Identifying effects		
	Identifying logical relationships		
	Identifying constraints		
Detection of SRS faults	Detecting SRS ambiguities	• CEGA-based ambiguities review list	Scalability was confirmed. Commercial tools are available.
	Validating A-CEG	• CEG validating algorithm • CEG validating rules	Not scalable. Domain knowledge is required to perform this sub-task.
Quantification of the impact of detected faults on software reliability	A-CEG revision	• A-CEG revision and B-CEG Construction Rules	Scalability was confirmed. No tools are required for these two sub-tasks
	B-CEG construction		
	Identifying failure-relevant inputs	• Failure-relevant identification algorithm • Generic A-CEG fault tree model	Scalability was confirmed. Ready for automation.
	BDD construction	• BDD techniques	Scalability was confirmed. Free tools are available.
	Calculating the occurrence probability of BDD's top node	• Recursive BDD's top node occurrence probability calculation algorithm	Scalability was confirmed. Tools were developed.

The size of the SRSs, the A-CEGs, and the cause-effect measures for these two experiments are summarized in Table 6-3.

---

[*] In this table, the "General CEG construction procedure and the general CEG construction guidelines", "CEGA-based ambiguities review list", and "BDD techniques" were developed by others rather than the author.

120

Table 6-3: A-CEGs and *CE(%)* for PACS and SXXX

Application	Size of SRS		Size of A-CEG				CE (%)
	Number of Pages	Number of sentences	Number of Causes	Number of Effects	Number of Logical relationships	Number of Constraints	
PACS	32	402	13	14	47	6	78.45
SXXX	289	3492	255	506	1608	30	85.71

The detailed results of Case Study A (for PACS) are given in Appendix C. For comparison purpose, the graphical expressions of A-CEG and B-CEG are also included in Appendix C, although they are not required by the experiment. Refer to our technical report [40] for the detailed results of Case Study B (for SXXX). In this section, we only report the high-level findings that are most relevant to our study objectives.

Finding 6-1: There is no obvious pattern in the distribution of detected faults against the CEG fault categories, as shown in Figure 6-1 and Figure 6-2.

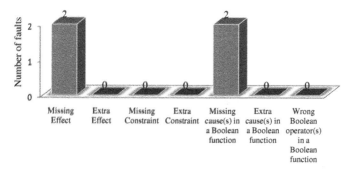

Figure 6-1: Distribution of Detected Faults in Case Study A (for PACS)

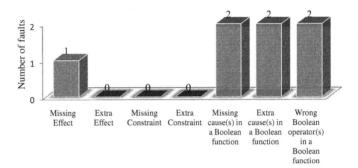

Figure 6-2: Distribution of Detected Faults in Case Study B (for SXXX)

Finding 6-2: An overwhelming presence of the identity logical relationship as the relationship between the cause and effect as shown in Figure 6-3 and Figure 6-4. This is a rather interesting finding since this might be useful in a future development of a tool.

Figure 6-3: Distribution of Logical Relationships in PACS' A-CEG

Figure 6-4: Distribution of Logical Relationships in SXXX's A-CEG

122

Finding 6-3: CEGA is effective in finding critical SRS faults (such as missing effects, wrong Boolean functions). Table 6-4 shows the number of (both critical and non-critical) faults detected in SRSs of PACS's and SXXX's and the efforts in detecting these faults. For information purpose, other SRS-based measurements results from our previous research [40][42] are included in Table 6-4, and illustrated in Figure 6-5 and Figure 6-6. These measurements include Completeness measurement, Defect Density measurement (using Requirements Inspection technique), and Requirements Traceability (RT) measurement. It should be noted that the human factor should be taken into account when interpreting the data on the table, because these four measurements were implemented by different persons.

Table 6-4: Number of Detected Faults vs. Efforts in Using SRS-related Measurements[5]

Application	CEGA		Requirements Completeness		Defect Density (Requirements inspection)[6]		Requirements Traceability[7]	
	Detected faults[8]	Effort, Staff-hr	Detected faults	Effort, Staff-hr	Detected faults	Effort, Staff-hr	Detected faults	Effort, Staff-hr
PACS	4 (3)	30	(not implemented)		9 (4)	40	2 (2)	35
SXXX	7 (7)	385.5	29 (4)	285.5	8 (5)	450	5 (3)	417
Average Staff-hour /fault	37.8		9.8		28.8		64.6	

---

[5] These measurements were implemented by different persons.
[6] Three inspectors and two moderators participated in PACS' SRS inspection. Two inspectors and one moderator participated in SXXX's SRS inspection.
[7] RT cannot be implemented until the end of coding phase.
[8] The numbers in parentheses on this table represent the numbers of critical SRS faults.

123

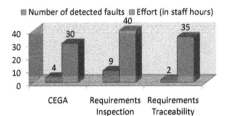

Figure 6-5: Number of Detected Faults vs. Effort for PACS

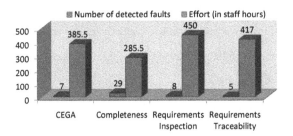

Figure 6-6: Number of Detected Faults vs. Effort for SXXX

Finding 6-4: Implementation of CEGA is very time-consuming. A considerable amount of time was spent in manually "parsing" the natural language SRS documents to construct an A-CEG and identifying SRS faults. This pattern is more obvious for an SRS with larger size (SXXX, in this case), as shown in Figure 6-7 and Figure 6-8. The time spent in identifying failure-relevant inputs and documenting results, which account for about 29% of the total effort in Case Study A and 23% in Case Study B, could be significantly reduced if automation tools had been available. We think that it is a relatively easy task to develop automation tools for reducing time spent in these two activities based on the automation-oriented algorithm proposed in Chapter 5 (see Section 5.3). However, it is very challenging to reduce the time spent in identifying

124

SRS faults since the effectiveness and efficiency of our CEGA-based SRS faults detection method is highly dependent on the ability of the person(s) using this method. Relevant resources, such as the user specification document, an end user, and so on, help the inspector improve his/her understanding of the system and identify faults in A-CEG. Training is also very helpful. Up to this point, it is not clear why A-CEG construction is so time-consuming and how to reduce the time spent in this activity. We will revisit this topic in Chapter 7.

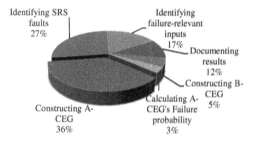

Figure 6-7: Distribution of Efforts in Case Study A (for PACS)

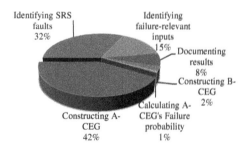

Figure 6-8: Distribution of Efforts in Case Study B (for SXXX)

Finding 6-5: Process of manually parsing SRS is error-prone. The effectiveness and efficiency of the CEGA measurement is highly dependent on the ability of the person exercising the measurement. It is highly recommended to assign an analyzer who knows the software very well to perform CEGA. This is mainly because it is not very easy to identify the true logical relationship between the causes and the constraints. Without prior knowledge of the system, the defects found through CEGA may not be correct and the final reliability prediction may not be very meaningful. A two-week-long training on the measurement and the domain knowledge is suggested before the inspector may carry out this measurement.

Finding 6-6: Metrics used early, such as the cause-effect measure, can aid in detection and correction of requirement faults that will lead to prevention of errors later in the life cycle. Finding these problematic areas in the requirements phase decreases the cost and prevents potential ripple effects from the changes, later in the development life cycle. The benefits of finding and correcting problems in the requirements phase has been demonstrated in the CEGA measurement, making a strong argument for pursuing this approach and building in reliability starting at the requirements phase.

Finding 6-7: The primitives (for example, the number of ambiguities in SRS) of the cause-effect measure are somewhat subjective. Repeatability of the cause-effect measure is not guaranteed. The domain knowledge and other subjective factors, to some extent, highly affect the inspector's judgment. Therefore, it is not appropriate for quantitatively assessing the quality of the SRS.

Finding 6-8: The reliability of this measurement usually under-estimates the reliability of the final source code since SRS faults may be detected and fixed during

126

later development phases. In practice, many of the ambiguities are identified and avoided during later development activities, such as design, coding, and testing.

6.4 Summary

The CEGA process is an old concept whose usage can be expended from merely a testing tool to a useful SRS validation and software reliability prediction tool.

The feasibility and scalability of our approach for early software reliability prediction has been examined against two real applications. Although feedbacks from the use of the proposed techniques have been encouraging, there are a number of areas that require further investigation.

According to the results of Case Study A and Case Study B, the feasibility of our approach is clearly confirmed and the scalability is the top issue that needs to be addressed. The scalability bottleneck of our approach lies in A-CEG construction and SRS faults detection, which account for more than 60% of the effort spent in implementing CEGA. The SRS faults detection requires domain knowledge. This part is less likely to be scalable. Although Case Study B showed that A-CEG construction using the general A-CEG construction guides was not scalable, we hypothesized that this was caused by the A-CEG contraction method (the general A-CEG construction guidelines). Two questions thus arise: "Is A-CEG construction scalable?" and "Are there other techniques that enable the scalability of A-CEG construction?" The answers to these questions are uncertain and can only become clear after extensive exploration of the nature of natural language SRSs.

Chapter 7: Exploration of the Scalability of A-CEG Construction

The starting point for our approach is the SRSs, which are typically expressed in the form of natural language statements. However, the uses of natural language for specifying requirements, which are so important for human communication, represent an obstacle to automatic analysis of SRS. Especially, the results of Case Study B (see Chapter 6) showed that one of the scalability barriers in our approach lied in A-CEG construction. We wanted to answer the question of whether A-CEG construction is scalable or not and attempted to provide solution(s), if possible, to overcome the scalability barrier caused by A-CEG construction. Because quantitative research requires large sample sizes and such a sampling was not feasible for our study, a qualitative case-study approach was employed to understand the nature of SRSs and A-CEG construction.

During the 2006 Fall Semester, we designed an empirical study (called *Empirical Study C*) and offered an independent study project titled "Rule-based A-CEG Elements Extraction for Software Requirements Documents" to senior undergraduates at The University of Maryland pursuing Electrical Engineering or Computer Engineering related majors. The focus of this project was to provide insight about characteristics of SRSs, determine the feasibility of automatic A-CEG elements extraction, and lay the ground work for developing SRS-specific information retrieval and/or text mining tools for automatic A-CEG elements extraction. The project was

128

part of Empirical Study C and served for educational purposes in accordance with regulations of the university.

This chapter reports the objectives, procedure, detailed findings and analysis pertinent to Empirical Study C.

7.1 Objectives

The objectives of Empirical Study C were:

1) to study the characteristics of SRS, gain insight into the nature of SRS related to A-CEG construction, and obtain empirical information that leads to greater understanding of A-CEG construction.

2) to observe, collect, and distill the "patterns" in A-CEG construction.

3) to identify factors impacting the A-CEG elements identification.

4) to explore method/rules to enhance the scalability of A-CEG construction.

5) to provide SRS writers with caveats to avoid some common problems found in SRSs which were specified in plain English. These problems not only add difficulties in identifying A-CEG elements, but also might lead to increased risks of unreliable software products.

While many generic and successful information retrieval and text mining techniques/tools exist, we wanted to explore the possibility of an SRS-specific method, and lay the ground work for developing information retrieval and/or text mining tools for automatic A-CEG elements extraction.

7.2 Methodology and Procedure

Empirical Study C had three steps:

Step 1: Experiment preparation.

Step 2: Implementation of the independent study project.

Step 3: Postmortem analysis and improvement.

7.2.1 Step 1: Experiment Preparation

We selected nine publicly available SRSs from different sectors (government, military, industry, and academia) used for Step 2. All of these SRSs were written in English and followed the format recommended by IEEE standard IEEE Std. 830-1998 [53]. These SRSs were:

SRS1: for MRC-II System [89], a system software as a replacement of the current MRC software providing a real-time robot control system for research in Computer-Integrated Surgery.

SRS2: for DPUFSW [90], a major component of the data processing unit in an airplane control software.

SRS3: for Long Range Advanced Scout Surveillance System [91], a system operable in both a stationary vehicle mounted configuration and in an autonomous dismounted configuration, which determines far target location coordinates, and provides a real-time target detection, recognition, and identification capability to the scout while permitting 24-hour adverse weather operations.

SRS4: for Qheadache [92], a computerized game that displays an interface used to solve a specific headache (puzzle).

130

SRS5: for The Graph Editor [93], an interactive application that allows the user to create, edit, layout, save, and print arbitrary graphs commonly used in software engineering. It uses the GXL graph notation standard for storing graphs to files.

SRS6: for "Software Engineering Tool" [94], an application for aiding the employees in the process of developing software.

SRS7: for the BTS (Bus Tracking System) [95], a system intended to assisting passengers with route planning, inform passengers of delayed busses, improve inter-bus transfers by informing bus drivers of connecting busses that are running behind schedule, help transit management produce accurate schedules, and help transit management allocate resources more efficiently.

SRS8: for FloristExchange [96], an e-commerce project that deals with selling flowers online. The resulting website contains a catalog, a shopping cart, and other features that enable the webmaster to effectively manage.

SRS9: for PICASSO [97], a major component of the Requirements Assistant System that provides an environment in which a group of developers can collaborate on the production of a set of software requirements.

Due to the time limitation, the student only worked on two pre-selected segments (about 10 pages in total) for each SRS, although the entire SRS was provided to him. Each SRS segment contained a complete section for a functional module, including "Input Section", "Processing Section", and "Output Section".

7.2.2 Step 2: Implementation of the Independent Study Project

This step lasted 16 weeks/3.5 months (not including two holiday breaks): 4 weeks

for the training sessions, 10 weeks for the SRS analysis sessions, and 2 weeks for the

finalization session. Figure 7-1 depicts the entire timeline for this step.

Figure 7-1: Timeline for Implementing the Independent Study Project

The focus of this step was to parse the selected SRSs segments and analyze how

the A-CEG elements, including the causes, effects, logical relationships, and

constraints, are found. The observation on the exploration process of the student in

Case Study A and Case Study B (see Chapter 6) suggests that A-CEG elements are

identified using the so-called "pattern-matching" approach [98]. One of the Natural

Language Processing (NLP) techniques closest to our research purposes Pattern-

matching is the act of checking for the presence of the constituents of a given pattern.

Pattern-matching is usually achieved on the basis of a set of pre-defined rules. A rule

is a generalized statement that describes what is and what is not an A-CEG element in

most or all cases. A "pattern" can be represented by a sequence of indicators which

would point us to A-CEG element(s). Indicators are signals to us that aid us identify

A-CEG elements in an SRS. These indicators are often verbs, nouns, prepositions that

seem to be associated with the rules. This study preferred the rule-based pattern-

132

matching approach for our research. Therefore, an attempt to establish a database of rules and indicators was also made in this step.

Before entering the SRS analysis sessions, the selected student was trained for 4 weeks on IEEE Std. 830-1998 [53] and knowledge of A-CEG construction. Self-study materials were assigned and help sessions were also provided to the student. Finally, the student was given a quiz in which he was asked to identify A-CEG elements in a sample SRS. After the quiz, we discussed with the student the list of known A-CEG elements and what A-CEG elements he had actually found. We accounted for correctly identified A-CEG elements (true positives), missed A-CEG elements (false negatives), and wrongly identified A-CEG elements (false positives), and analyzed the cause of the false negatives and false positives, and tried to identify improvements[9]. All of these steps were taken to ensure that the student had mastered the technique on A-CEG construction.

After we were convinced that the student was capable of performing the SRS analysis tasks, Empirical Study C was shifted to SRS analysis sessions. There were 10 such sessions, each of which lasted one week. Each session consisted of an individual analysis of SRS performed by the student (about 6 hours), and a following face-to-face discussion (about 2 hours) joined by the student and the author.

The student first followed the workflow shown in Figure 7-2 to extract rules and indicators for identification of A-CEG elements.

––––––––––––––––––––

[9] The student got 70% for Accuracy, 80% for Recall, and 84% for Precision in the quiz. See Chapter 8 for definitions of Accuracy, Recall, and Precision.

133

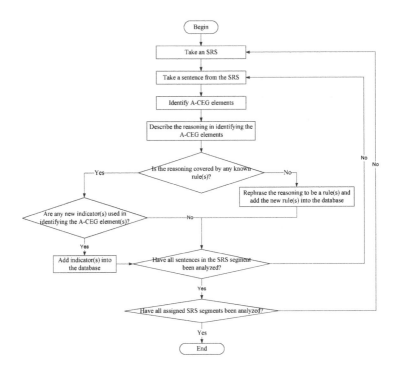

Figure 7-2: Workflow for Extracting Rules and Indicators for identification of A-

CEG Elements

The determination to add new rule(s) into the database is somewhat subjective. The student made judgments primarily based on common sense. To ensure the quality of experimental results, we asked the student to record down information pertinent to his judgments, such as the detected CEG element(s), and the reasoning that led to the identification of the CEG element(s), the extracted rules and indicators, and so on. He was also required to document any issues that he had encountered during the individual session.

134

He then illustrated the documented results and worked through the collected rules and indicators with the author during the discussion session. In addition, problems, difficulties, and other issues regarding performance of the analysis tasks were proposed and discussed as well. As such, we could make sure that the project was on the right track.

After completing all of the ten SRS analysis sessions, the student was asked to finalize the results (including the database containing the extracted rules and indicators) and submit a report for the independent study project. The database is expressed in the form of a Microsoft Excel® worksheet containing related information, such as the SRS segment, the page number and sentence number on the SRS segment, the detected CEG element(s), the reasoning that led to the identification of the CEG element(s), the rule(s) that was applied or proposed to extract the CEG element(s), and/or the extracted indicator(s), and so on.

There were quite a few implied A-CEG elements (especially causes and logical relationships) in the parsed SRS segments. We were very cautious to make a rule when implication was used, since the process by which the implied A-CEG element was found was rather subjective.

Note that there were two analysis sessions assigned for SRS4 (including a regular and a re-work session) because of the degree of difficulty and peculiarity of the text. The difficulties with analyzing SRS4 the first time can be attributed to the fact that it contained a large number of implied causes and the student had no idea how to handle implied A-CEG elements.

7.2.3 Step 3: Postmortem Analysis and Improvement

In this step, the author further improved the rules and indicators obtained in Step 2 by making the rules more general and unified, and distilled a set of A-CEG Construction Rules. Moreover, the potential influencing factors for both A-CEG construction and the use of the A-CEG Construction Rules were identified and analyzed. Suggestions that would ease the task of A-CEG construction and help avoid some common problems in SRSs were also made during this step.

The process used to distill the A-CEG Construction Rules is shown in Figure 7-3. Table 7-1 shows two items in the rules and indicators database that were used to develop Rule 7-1 (see Page 140) and Rule 7-11 (see Page 147).

Table 7-1: Example Items Used to Develop Rule 7-1 and Rule 7-11

Item No.	SRS Segment No.	Page No.	Sentence No.	Detected CEG element(s)	Reasoning	Indicator(s)	Applied/Proposed Rule(s)
⋮	⋮	⋮	⋮	⋮	⋮	⋮	⋮
5	SRS1	7	3	The sentence "The API shall provide query commands for any external sensors" contains an effect "The API provide query…"	The action word "provide" signifies an event. The word "API" indicates that the action is performed by the system under study. The object of the event is something external.	API; shall; provide; external sensor.	• An action word should indicate an event. • An event performed by the system under study should be an effect. • A verb should be regarded as an action word.
⋮	⋮	⋮	⋮	⋮	⋮	⋮	⋮
51	SRS3	5	4	The sentence "The product must count and display the number of the user' actions" contains two effect: "the product counts …" and "the product displays…"	The action word "count" and "display" signify two events. The word "product" indicates that action is performed by the system under study. The object of the events is the number of user's actions.	product; must; count; and display; the number of user' action.	• An action word should indicate an event. • An "and" between two action words should indicate two events. • An event(s) performed by "product" should be an effect. • A verb should be regarded as an action word.
⋮	⋮	⋮	⋮	⋮	⋮	⋮	⋮

136

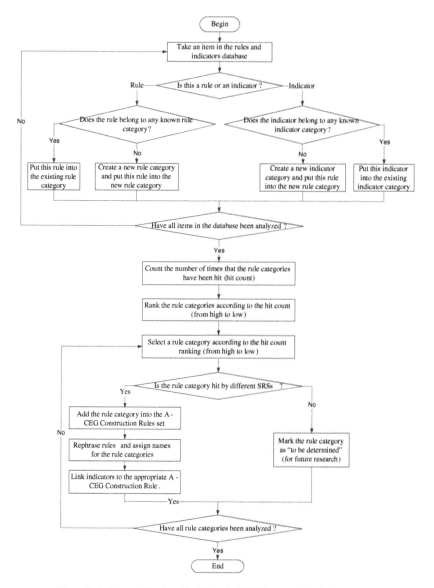

Figure 7-3: Process Used to Distill the A-CEG Construction Rules

137

It should be noted that we did not define any strict criteria for classifying rules/indicator categories. In addition, there might be other better ways to extract and express the rules for A-CEG construction based on the database obtained in Step 2.

7.3 Results and Discussion

7.3.1 The Database of Rules and Indicators for A-CEG Elements Identification

Through Step 2, we acquired a fairly large database containing rules and indicators for identification of A-CEG elements. Below are the figures (Figure 7-4 and Figure 7-5) summarizing the numbers of rules and indicators we found for each SRS segment.

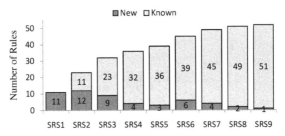

Figure 7-4: Number of Rules Extracted from Selected SRSs

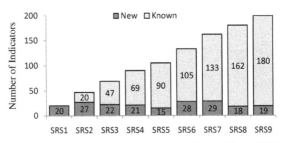

Figure 7-5: Number of Indicators Extracted from Selected SRSs

138

Figure 7-4 shows that in the first 6 SRS documents we developed a good amount of rules; after that the identification of rules dropped off. Figure 7-5 shows that the indicators stay fairly constant across all SRS'. These statistics suggest that we would just continue adding indicators to our list and that on the other hand few new rules would be found for the database if we had analyzed more SRS segments.

7.3.2 The A-CEG Construction Rules

The A-CEG Construction Rules were developed and distilled on the basis of a database of rules and indicators obtained from Step 2. These rules often depend on prepositions, punctuation, and sentence structure. Additionally, very often they need to be used in conjunction with indicators to determine A-CEG elements. These indicators were loosely grouped to maximize hit potential. Table 7-2 shows the mapping of rules in the database to the A-CEG Construction Rules listed in this section. Refer to Appendix D for brief descriptions of the rules in the database.

Table 7-2: Mapping of the Database's Rules to the A-CEG Construction Rules[10]

Index of Database's Rules	Index of the A-CEG Construction Rules											
	7-1	7-2	7-3	7-4	7-5	7-6	7-7	7-8	7-9	7-10	7-11	7-12
1	✓	✗	✗	✗	✗	✗	✗	✗	✗	✗	✗	✗
2	✓	✗	✗	✗	✗	✗	✗	✗	✗	✗	✗	✗
3	✗	✗	✗	✗	✓	✗	✗	✗	✗	✗	✗	✗
4	✗	✗	✗	✗	✓	✗	✓	✗	✗	✗	✗	✗
5	✗	✗	✗	✗	✗	✗	✗	✗	✗	✗	✗	✗
6	✗	✓	✗	✗	✗	✗	✗	✗	✗	✗	✗	✗
7	✗	✗	✗	✗	✓	✓	✗	✗	✗	✗	✗	✗

[10] Table legend: ✓ = mapped; ✗ = not mapped.

139

Index of Database's Rules	Index of the A-CEG Construction Rules											
	7-1	7-2	7-3	7-4	7-5	7-6	7-7	7-8	7-9	7-10	7-11	7-12
8	✓	✗	✗	✗	✗	✗	✗	✗	✓	✗	✗	✗
9	✗	✗	✗	✗	✓	✗	✗	✗	✗	✗	✗	✗
10	✓	✗	✗	✗	✗	✗	✗	✗	✗	✗	✗	✗
11	✗	✗	✓	✗	✗	✗	✗	✗	✗	✗	✗	✗
12	✗	✗	✗	✗	✗	✗	✗	✗	✗	✗	✗	✗
13	✗	✗	✗	✗	✓	✓	✗	✗	✗	✗	✗	✗
14	✗	✓	✗	✗	✗	✗	✗	✗	✗	✗	✗	✗
15	✗	✗	✗	✗	✓	✗	✗	✗	✗	✗	✗	✗
16	✗	✗	✗	✓	✗	✗	✗	✗	✗	✗	✗	✗
17	✗	✗	✗	✗	✗	✗	✗	✗	✗	✓	✗	✗
18	✓	✗	✗	✗	✗	✗	✗	✗	✗	✗	✗	✓
19	✗	✗	✗	✗	✗	✗	✗	✓	✗	✗	✗	✗
20	✗	✗	✗	✗	✓	✗	✗	✗	✗	✗	✗	✗
21	✗	✗	✓	✓	✗	✗	✗	✗	✗	✗	✗	✗
22	✗	✗	✗	✗	✗	✗	✗	✗	✗	✗	✗	✗
23	✗	✓	✗	✗	✗	✗	✗	✗	✗	✗	✗	✗
24	✗	✗	✗	✗	✗	✗	✗	✗	✗	✗	✗	✗
25	✓	✗	✗	✗	✗	✗	✗	✗	✓	✗	✓	✗
26	✗	✗	✗	✗	✓	✗	✗	✗	✗	✗	✗	✗
27	✗	✗	✗	✗	✓	✗	✗	✗	✗	✗	✗	✗
28	✗	✗	✗	✗	✗	✗	✗	✗	✗	✗	✗	✗
29	✓	✗	✗	✗	✗	✗	✗	✗	✗	✗	✗	✗
30	✗	✗	✗	✗	✗	✗	✗	✓	✗	✗	✗	✗
31	✗	✗	✗	✗	✗	✗	✗	✗	✗	✗	✗	✗
32	✓	✗	✗	✗	✗	✗	✗	✗	✓	✗	✗	✗
33	✗	✗	✗	✗	✗	✗	✗	✗	✗	✗	✗	✗
34	✗	✗	✗	✗	✓	✓	✗	✗	✗	✗	✗	✗
35	✗	✗	✗	✗	✗	✗	✗	✗	✗	✗	✗	✗
36	✗	✗	✓	✗	✗	✗	✗	✗	✗	✗	✗	✗
37	✗	✗	✗	✓	✗	✗	✗	✗	✗	✗	✗	✗
38	✗	✗	✗	✗	✗	✗	✗	✗	✗	✗	✗	✗
39	✗	✗	✗	✗	✗	✗	✗	✗	✗	✗	✗	✗
40	✓	✗	✗	✗	✗	✗	✗	✗	✓	✗	✗	✗
41	✗	✗	✗	✗	✗	✗	✗	✗	✗	✗	✗	✗
42	✓	✗	✗	✗	✗	✗	✗	✗	✗	✗	✗	✓
43	✗	✗	✗	✗	✗	✗	✗	✗	✗	✗	✗	✗
44	✗	✓	✗	✗	✗	✗	✗	✗	✗	✗	✗	✗
45	✗	✗	✗	✗	✗	✗	✗	✗	✗	✓	✗	✗
46	✗	✗	✗	✗	✗	✗	✗	✗	✗	✗	✗	✗
47	✗	✗	✗	✗	✗	✗	✗	✗	✗	✗	✗	✗
48	✓	✗	✗	✗	✗	✗	✗	✗	✓	✗	✗	✗
49	✗	✗	✗	✗	✗	✗	✗	✗	✗	✗	✗	✗

Index of Database's Rules	Index of the A-CEG Construction Rules											
	7-1	7-2	7-3	7-4	7-5	7-6	7-7	7-8	7-9	7-10	7-11	7-12
50	✕	✕	✕	✕	✕	✕	✓	✕	✕	✕	✕	✕
51	✕	✕	✕	✓	✕	✕	✕	✕	✕	✕	✕	✕
52	✕	✕	✕	✕	✕	✕	✕	✕	✕	✕	✕	✕

Rule 7-1: Action-word Rule (for identifying events)

An action word in a requirements statement indicates at least an event (or events, if Rule 7-2 is applicable).

Action words are those that are used to specify control of physical input/output exchanges in a program, or implementation of application actions, such as reading a screen, submitting a query to a database, opening or closing a file. An action word is usually a verb which indicates some activities performed. Typical action words include:

call	calculate	check	close
create	delete	display	grant
halt	Initiate	notify	open
prevent	print	prohibit	prompt
protect	provide	quit	read
remove	require	reset	retrieve
return	save	send	set
share	store	transfer	transmit
use	validate	verify	write

Example: "The function displays the message on the screen" is identified as an event because it contains "displays" that is regarded as an action word.

Rule 7-2: Atomic-event Rule

An event must be a non-divisible activity. In other words, a complex activity, typically signified by an "and" or an "or", must be decomposed into several atomic events. All events should be mutually exclusive in the sense that no one event is part of another.

Example: "If the user presses down the right mouse key and then press left mouse key, ..." contains two events "the user presses down the right mouse key" and "then (the user) press left mouse key".

Rule 7-3: Lowest-level-event Rule

In a cause-effect graph, an event must be the lowest level of activity. If an event is reiterated by other lower level events, the following steps are applied:

1. This event should not be identified as a complex (non-atomic) event.
2. This event should be replaced by the lowest-level events.
3. All lowest-level events should be identified as events.
4. The constraint EXCLUSIVE should be applied to these lowest-level events.

Example: "The user provides the input from the keyboard. There are four options provided by the user: option 1, option 2, option 3, and option 4."

In this case, "the user provides the input from the keyboard" should not be identified as an event. Instead, "the user provides option 1", "the user provides option 2", "the user provides option 3", and "the user provides option 4" are identified as four distinct events. Besides, the EXCLUSIVE constraint is applied among these four events.

142

Rule 7-4: No-duplicate-event Rule

In a cause-effect graph, every event is unique. In other words, duplicate events should be removed from a cause-effect graph.

Rule 7-5: Logical-relationship-pattern Rule

The logical relationships among events are identified by matching the sentence to one of the following four basic patterns:

1. **IDENTITY pattern**: IF event a THEN event b.
2. **NOT pattern**: IF NOT event a THEN event b.
3. **AND pattern**: IF event a_1 AND event a_2 THEN event b.
4. **OR pattern**: IF event a_1 OR event a_2 THEN event b.

The functional requirements specifications can be casted into sentences of one of the above forms. Therefore, the problem of identifying logical relationships should be one of finding the keywords: IF, THEN, AND, OR, and NOT. Unfortunately we have to deal with the real world of specifications and specification writers, where clarity ranges from elusive, through esoteric, into incomprehensible. It takes intelligence to disentangle intentions that are hidden by ambiguities inherent in English and by poor English usage.

Here is a sample of phrases that have been or can be used (and abused) for the indicators we need. Be aware that this is *not* a list of recommended synonyms for specification writers. Several entries appear in more than one sub-list indicating a source of danger. Besides, there are other dangerous phrases, such as "respectively," "similarly," "conversely," "and so forth," and "etc."

143

IF

based on	based upon	because	but
if	if and when	only if	only when
provided that	when	when or if	whenever

THEN

consequently	implies that	infers that	means that
shall	should	then	will
would			

AND

all	and	as well as	both
but	in conjunction with	coincidental with	consisting of
comprising	either	or	furthermore
in addition to	including	jointly	moreover
mutually	plus	together with	total
with			

OR

and	and if	then	and/or
alternatively	any of	anyone of	as well as
but	case	contrast	depending upon
each	either	either . . . or	except if
conversely	failing that	furthermore	in addition to
nor	not only . . . but	although	other than
otherwise	or	or else	on the other hand

144

plus

NOT

but	but not	by contrast	besides
contrary	conversely	contrast	except if
excluding	excepting	fail	failing
less	neither	never	no
not	other than		

Rule 7-6: Single-If Rule

For a group of expressions in form of "If *Expression 1*, then *Expression 2*; otherwise *Expression 3*", the following steps are applied:

1. *Expression 1* consists of at least an event.

2. *Expression 2* consists of at least an event.

3. *Expression 3* consists of at least an event.

4. Omission of *Expression 2* or *Expression 3* is regarded as a fault.

Rule 7-7: Nesting-If Rule

For a group of expressions in form of "If *Expression 1-1*, then *Expression 2-1*; If *Expression 1-2*, (then) *Expression 2-2*; If *Expression 1-3*, (then) *Expression 2-3*; ...", the following steps are applied:

1. Expression 1-1, Expression 1-2, Expression 1-3, ..., consists of at least an event, respectively.

2. Expression 2-1, Expression 2-2, Expression 2-3, ..., consists of at least an event, respectively.

3. Constraint EXCLUSIVE should be applied to event(s) in Expression 1-1 and event(s) in Expression 1-2, Expression 1-3, etc.

4. Omission of any of *Expression 2-1, 2-2, 2-3*, etc., is regarded as an SRS fault.

Example: "If the choice is '1', the function Range will be initiated. If the choice is '2', the function Speed will be initiated. If the choice is '3', the function Trajectory will be initiated. If the choice is '4', the function quits. For all other options the function 'Error' will be initiated."

In this case, there are ten events, including "the choice is '1'", "the choice is '2'", "the choice is '3'", "the choice is '4'", "all other options", "the function Range will be initiated", "the function Speed will be initiated", "the function Trajectory will be initiated", "the function quits", and "the function 'Error' will be initiated". Besides, the constraint EXCLUSIVE is applied to the first five events.

Rule 7-8: Sequentially-triggered-event Rule

For sequential events, e_1, e_2, ..., e_n, that are triggered by an event (either atomic or non-atomic), e, the following steps are applied:

1. The IDENTITY logical relationships should be applied to the triggering event and the triggered events in form of $e_1 := e$, $e_2 := e$, ..., $e_n := e$.

2. A series of REQUIRE constraints should be applied to the triggered events in form of REQUIRE $(e_n, e_{n-1},)$, REQUIRE $(e_{n-1}, e_{n-2},)$, ..., REQUIRE $(e_2, e_1,)$.

Example: *If event A leads to four events, event 1, event 2, event 3, and event 4 and these four events should occur one after another, the following logical relationships and constraints should be applied to them:*

event 1:= event A
event 2:= event A   REQUIRE (*event 4, event 3*),
event 3:= event A   REQUIRE (*event 3, event 2*)
event 4:= event A   REQUIRE (*event 2, event 1*)

Alternatively, the A-CEG snippet for this requirements segment can be graphically expressed as follows:

Rule 7-9: External-Actor Rule (for identifying causes)

An event performed by external entities is a cause. An external entity (called *external actor*) is a human or external system/function/application that communicates with the system, function, or application under discussion. Typical indicators for external actor(s) are:

alarm	card	card-reader	client
CPU	database	file	keyboard
LED	message	microprocessor	monitor
RAM	record	screen	supervisor
timer	user		

147

Example: *"If the input value is greater than 0 and in the format F10.4"* contains two events *"the input value is greater than 0"* and *"the input value is in the format F10.4".* These two events are identified as causes because their actor is the user who provides the software with the input values.

Rule 7-10: Is-Are Rule (for identifying causes)

Even without using any action words, descriptions on the status/conditions of external entities using "is" or "are" should signify a cause(s).

Example: *"If the input value is greater than 0 and in the format F10.4"* contains two causes *"the input value is greater than 0"* and *"the input value is in the format F10.4".*

Rule 7-11: Internal-Actor Rule (for identifying effects)

An event performed by the function under discussion (called *internal actor*) is an effect. Typical indicators for internal actor(s) are:

this algorithm	this application	this function	this module
this system			

Example: *"This function should initiate Function Interface after its execution"* is identified as an effect.

Rule 7-12: Default Actor Rule (for identifying causes)

If not specified, an event by default is performed by the function under discussion and thus is identified as an effect.

148

Example: *"the projection angle is validated".*

In this case, there is an action word "validate". According to Rule 7-1, "the projection angle is validated" is identified as an event. Besides, there is no explicit actor mentioned in the statement. According to Rule 7-12, this event is identified as an effect.

The suggested workflow for using the A-CEG Construction Rules is shown in Figure 7-6.

149

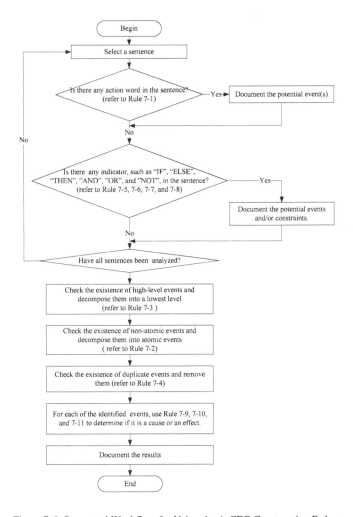

Figure 7-6: Suggested Workflow for Using the A-CEG Construction Rules

In addition to the A-CEG Construction Rules presented previously, the following

guidelines, which were also summarized in our previous research [40] (to be printed), are helpful for CEG construction:

- To identify causes, read the specification carefully, underlining words or phrases that describe causes. Any distinct input condition or equivalence class [11] of input conditions should be considered causes. Only functional events in the specification are considered. Each cause is assigned to a unique number. None of the descriptive specifications are considered in identifying causes.

- Effects can be identified by reading the specification carefully and underlining words or phrases that describe effects. Only functional events in the specification are considered. To avoid redundancy, all the descriptive specifications are not considered in identifying effects. Each effect is assigned to a unique identifier.

- The logical relationship between causes and effects can be identified by analyzing the semantic content of the specification linking the causes with the effects. Those keywords like "not", "or", "and" etc. usually act as indicators of logical relationships. Other words having the logical meaning, such as "both", "neither" also need to be paid much attention to. The logical relationships are mainly found in functional specifications. However they could be found in some descriptive specifications. In order to identify all logical relationships

---

[11] An equivalence class is a portion of a component's input or output domains for which the component's behavior is assumed to be the same from the component's specification [45].

151

between causes and effects, both functional and descriptive specifications need to be analyzed.

- The external constraints among causes can be identified by checking for the occurrence of related causes specified in SRS. The external constraints among effects can be identified by checking for the occurrence of related effects specified in SRS. As with the logical relationships, the external constraints could be specified in both functional specifications and descriptive specifications. In order to identify all external constraints, both functional and descriptive specifications need to be analyzed.

The database and the A-CEG Construction Rules set had showed promise of pointing and extracting the correct A-CEG elements when we tentatively applied them to several SRSs. However, there are multiple issues that need to be addressed:

- The database is a small start and only scratched the surface. As expected, the database is extremely limited in the way of having enough indicators to be adequate when covering SRSs that have not been analyzed yet.
- We need to establish a priority system or algorithm to determine which rules are used first and smartly combine the rules in order to get the most accurate result.
- For indicators in the database to be more effective, it would seem desirable to develop a domain-specific list of indicators and their synonyms to strengthen the accuracy of identifying A-CEG elements using our approach. This is especially true for action words used to identify events. For example, the

152

following list of action words is commonly found in most privacy-policies-related functional requirements in the internet security domain:

advise	aggregate	allow	collect
comply	customize	disallow	discipline
disclose	ensure	improve	keep
limit	notify	opt-in	opt-out
prevent	prohibit	protect	provide
recognize	remove	report	require
retrieve	sell	send	share
store	track	transmit	transfer
use			

7.3.3 Potential Influencing Factors of A-CEG Construction

There were several major problems that were impeding efficient identification of A-CEG elements in this experiment:

1. Redundancy: This issue mostly stems from the overviews and general description section, in which author(s) of an SRS reiterate the algorithms/procedure for some functional requirements. While overviews and general description in an SRS are important for the understanding of the reader, they often act as "trouble-makers" (leading to problems such as redundancy and inconsistence) rather than "trouble-shooters". Distinguishing between those and the real functional requirements can be difficult and may be a major obstacle precluding the A-CEG Construction

153

Rules from becoming efficient. This could also be a potential obstacle for automatic extraction of A-CEG elements.

2. Ambiguities: It might sound surprising that CEGA itself is a victim of SRS ambiguities, even when CEGA has a proven powerful ability in detecting SRS ambiguities. However, it is true that SRS ambiguities prevent the A-CEG Construction Rules from becoming efficient. They are also obstacles for automatic extraction of A-CEG elements.

3. Incompleteness/implication. This issue usually arises when functional requirements are implicitly stated. Often the authors of SRSs do not feel the need to explicitly express causes, while the effects are usually stated well. For instance, SRS4 that we had trouble with had a lot of implied causes. In this situation we often had to either imply a cause, or imply a relationship to a previously found cause. In addition, there were quite a few implied logical relationships in the parsed SRS segments. Besides, it was extremely hard to find an explicitly expressed logical relationship when the procedure of an algorithm/function was described in a chronological manner. This was especially true when the descriptions were based on dataflow, where one had to imply the relationship between a found cause(s) and effect(s). The logical relationship was just shown by sequential descriptions, which did not give us a true explicitly stated relationship.

4. Understandability of identified events. This issue is usually related to inappropriate words and/or phrases used for the statements of functional

154

requirements. While we may be able to extract some of those that are not easily understood, we do so with risk of identifying incorrect A-CEG elements. Even when the right A-CEG elements are extracted, it would not have a lot of meaning to the reader of the graph, if he/she did not read the entire SRS. This will significantly reduce the benefits from the CEGA approach.

In addition, our observations in this experiment suggest that several variables might have important influence on performing A-CEG construction as well as the use of the A-CEG construction Rules:

- The SRS' writing style. The presentation style of the specifications is a critical factor in the ease of A-CEG construction. A specification written as a logical design document is not suitable for A-CEG construction. The measure of the SRS' writing style is defined in Chapter 8.

- The SRS' application type, which is defined in Chapter 8.

- Complexity of the system under study.

- The size of SRS (in terms of the number of sentences).

- The standard that the SRS follows to organize the content.

- Person-related factors, including:

    a. Capability of the person performing the task.

    b. Domain knowledge on the system under study.

    c. Prior industrial experience or other job related experiences in writing requirements.

d. Educational background, such as majors of university degrees, and level of education (BS, MS, Ph.D.).

Especially, it is important to understand the variations among the individuals that make them more or less effective in A-CEG construction and identifying the characteristics that make an individual particularly effective.

7.3.4 Suggestions for Writing an SRS

Natural language's extensive vocabulary and commonly understood syntax facilitate communication and make it an inviting choice to express requirements. The informality of the language also makes it relatively easy to specify high-level general requirements when precise details are not yet known. However, because of differences among formal, colloquial, and popular definitions of words and phrases and the effort required to produce detailed information, these same attributes also contribute to documentation problems. The use of natural language to prescribe complex, dynamic systems has at least three common and severe problems: ambiguity, inaccuracy, and inconsistency. These problems not only add difficulties in identifying A-CEG elements, but also might lead to increased risks of unreliable software products. Fortunately, these defects can be prevented through a more disciplined and consistent approach to document design, formulation of specification statements, and selection of key words and phrases.

Poorly structured specification statements result in confusing requirements that are prone to incorrect interpretations. Start rewriting the specification by getting rid of ambiguous terms, words, and phrases and expressing it all as a long list of "IF . . .

THEN. . ." statements. The main point of translating the specification into unambiguous English that uses "IF", "THEN", "AND", "OR", and "NOT" is that this form is less likely to be misinterpreted.

The use of imprecise terms usually indicates that the specifications author was either lazy, incompetent, or did not have sufficient time to determine the exact requirements. Some writers seem to be afraid that their audience will be bored or will think them lazy if they use simple words and repeat themselves. When writing documents or software, being too fancy complicates things and make the resulting products hard to understand.

Specifications could be further strengthened through a better selection of words and phrases. The precise meaning of many words and phrases depends entirely on the context in which they are used. Attention must be given to the role of each word and phrase when formulating specification statements. Words and phrases that are carelessly selected or carelessly placed produce statements that are ambiguous and imprecise. The simplest word that is appropriate to its intended purpose in the specification is the one to use. In particular, we have the following suggestions for writing an SRS:

- Use the correct imperative and use it consistently. For instance, the word "shall" prescribes, "will" describes, "must" and "must not" constrain, and "should" suggests.

- Avoid weak phrases such as "as a minimum," "be able to," "capable of," and "not limited to." These phrases are subject to different interpretations and also set the stage for future changes to the requirements.

- Do not use words or terms that give the reader an option regarding the extent to which the requirement is to be satisfied, such as "may," "if required," "as appropriate," or "if practical."

- Avoid using immaterial words or phrases, such as "independent of", "regardless", "irrespective", "irrelevant", "regardless", "but not if", and "whether or not".

- Do not use generalities when numbers are required, for example, "large," "rapid," "many," "timely," "most," and "close." Avoid imprecise words that have relative meanings such as "easy," "normal," "adequate," or "effective."

- If a specification statement contains three or more punctuation marks, it probably needs to be restructured.

7.4 Summary

In this chapter, we focus on exploring the scalability of A-CEG construction. We present an empirical experiment designed to understand how an undergraduate developed A-CEG elements and his exploration process. We briefly describe our goals and the experiment procedure, and give clues about data collection and analysis. We obtain a database of rules and indicators for identification of A-CEG elements and finally develop the A-CEG Construction Rules set on the basis of the database. We conclude with lessons learnt from this experiment and discuss the potential influencing factors on A-CEG construction. Caveats to avoid some common problems found in the practice of specifying SRSs were also discussed. Putting these suggestions into practice not only eases the task of identifying A-CEG elements, but also avoids some common problematic requirements and finally leads to reduced risks of unreliable software products.

Even when the A-CEG Construction Rules set is still open for criticism and improvement, we believe that using the indicators together with the A-CEG Construction Rules will maximize the possibility of recognizing a good amount of A-CEG elements. We also feel sure that A-CEG construction using our approach is somewhat automatic.

Chapter 8: Validation of the Usability of the A-CEG Construction Rules

A methodology must be usable for people other than its developer and must be able to be incorporated into practice for its users. Usability is usually employed for measuring the capability of a methodology to be understood, learned, used, and attractive to the user, or the effort needed for use, when used under specified conditions. We wanted to explore the usability of the A-CEG Construction Rules. Moreover, we were very interested in investigating whether the rules set succeeds in its goals of providing the same or improved benefits for A-CEG construction, with what cost, and under what circumstances it makes the most sense. A controlled experiment seemed the ideal way to provide empirical evidence for our research interest.

During the Spring 2007 Semester, we conducted a small-scale controlled experiment (called *Experiment D*) at University of Maryland with the intention

1) To compare and hence evaluate how well the A-CEG Construction Rules set performs in comparison to other A-CEG construction methods. Especially, we wanted to compare the A-CEG Construction Rules set to the widely used general A-CEG construction guidelines.

2) To formulate hypotheses about the relationships between other factors (such as SRS' writing style and application type) and the effectiveness/efficiency of

an A-CEG constructor in identifying A-CEG elements (including the causes, effects, logical relationships, and constraints).

This chapter provides the pertinent information about the experiment. It describes the definitions, research questions, hypotheses, the variables measured, the experimental design (including the subjects, experiment materials, and procedures), the data collection process, threats to validity, and finally a detailed discussion of the experimental results.

8.1 *Definitions*

The following definitions are used throughout the remainder of this chapter.

Definition 8-1: Usability

Usability is a term used to denote the ease with which people can employ a technique in order to achieve a particular goal. According to Shneiderman [99], usability mainly observes learnability, effectiveness, efficiency, and user satisfaction.

Definition 8-2: Learnability

Learnability is a measure of how rapidly a new user can start using the technique and also how an infrequent user can re-learn the technique after periods of not using it. Learning time is the typical measure for learnability.

In this study, we measured the learning time by adding the time spent in training sessions, time spent during the help sessions and the time spent on study materials. The time spent on study materials was recorded from the log sheets of the students.

Definition 8-3: Effectiveness

Effectiveness is the measure of how easily a user can achieve basic tasks according to specific goals. Effectiveness is a measure of strategic performance: the ability to create an intended outcome.

In this study, the effectiveness of a subject in identifying A-CEG elements is evaluated by three indicators: accuracy, recall, and precision. All of these three indicators are calculated based on the confusion matrix, a typical result counting technique. A confusion matrix contains information about actual and predicted classifications done by a subject, as shown in Figure 8-1.

		Predicted	
		Positive ("yes")	Negative ("no")
Actual	Positive ("yes")	True Positive *(TP)*	False Negative *(FN)*
	Negative ("no")	False Positive *(FP)*	True Negative *(TN)*

Figure 8-1: Confusion Matrix

True Positives (*TP*s), True Negatives (*TN*s), False Positives (*FP*s), and False Negatives (*FN*s), are the four different possible outcomes of a single prediction for a two-class case with classes "positive" ("yes") and "negative" ("no"). A false positive, *FP*, is when the outcome is incorrectly classified as "positive" (or "yes") when it is in fact "negative" (or "no"). A false negative, *FN*, is when the outcome is incorrectly classified as negative when it is in fact positive. True positives and true negatives are obviously correct classifications.

Definition 8-4: Accuracy

162

The *Accuracy* is the proportion of the total number of predictions that were correct. It is determined using the below equation:

$$\text{Accuracy} = \frac{TPs + TNs}{TPs + FPs + TNs + FNs}$$

(Eq. 8-1)

In this study, the accuracy is the primary measure of effectiveness. However, the accuracy determined using (Eq. 8-1) may not be an adequate effectiveness measure when the number of negative cases is much greater than the number of positive cases. Suppose there are 1000 cases, 995 of which are negative cases and 5 of which are positive cases. If the system classifies them all as negative, the accuracy would be 99.5%, even though the classifier missed all positive cases. Accounting for this, the recall and precision are included as subsidiary measures of effectiveness.

Definition 8-5: Recall

The *Recall* or *true positive rate* is the proportion of positive cases that were correctly identified, as calculated using the equation below:

$$\text{Recall} = \frac{TPs}{TPs + FNs}$$

(Eq. 8-2)

Definition 8-6: Precision

Precision is the proportion of the predicted positive cases that were correct, as calculated using the equation below:

$$\text{Precision} = \frac{TPs}{TPs + FPs}$$

(Eq. 8-3)

Definition 8-7: Efficiency

163

Efficiency is a measure of how fast a user can achieve goals. It is an operationally-oriented measure of productivity. The efficiency is determined using the below equation:

$$\text{Efficiency} = \frac{TPs + TNs}{Effort} \qquad \text{(Eq. 8-4)}$$

The time to find the A-CEG elements was considered as the measure of effort. This value was directly available from the log-sheets collected in the experiment.

Definition 8-8: User Satisfaction

User satisfaction, also called *User Appeal* or *Subjective Satisfaction*, is the degree to which users like the method. This is a more "subjective" factor which refers to attitude, perceptions, and feelings that a user experiences when interacting with a technique.

In this study, we divide the user satisfaction into five categories, with Category 1 being the most satisfactory and Category 5 the least satisfactory.

Definition 8-9: SRS Writing Style

Stylometry quantifies aspects of writing style. This study adopts Labbe's Relative Inter-textual Distance [100] as the SRS stylometric characterization since its accuracy in text classification was confirmed by applications [101].

The Relative inter-textual distance measures the degree of proximity between texts. The relative inter-textual distance between text A and B is:

164

$$\delta_{(A,B)} = \frac{\sum_{i \in (A,B)} |F_{iA} - E_{iA}|}{\sum_{i \in A} F_{iA} + \sum_{i \in B} E_{iA}}$$ (Eq. 8-5)

where

$\delta_{(A,B)}$ = the relative inter-textual distance between text A and B.

F_{iA} = the absolute frequency of type i in text A.

E_{iA} = Expected frequency of type i in text A occurring in text B,

$$E_{iA} = F_{iB} \times \frac{N_A}{N_B} \quad .$$

F_{iB} = the absolute frequency of type i in text B.

N_A = size of text A, in number of tokens.

N_B = size of text B, in number of tokens $(N_B > N_A)$.

The values of relative distance vary evenly between 0 and 1.

To determine an appropriate threshold relative inter-textual distance to classify SRS' writing style into two levels, we conducted a preliminary study by taking the following steps:

1) Collect a set of publicly available SRSs that follow IEEE Std. 830-1998 [53]. Forty eight SRSs were selected in this study, including the eight SRSs that were used in our previous research. These eight SRSs were written by a Ph.D. graduate student using a consistent writing style, i.e. consistently using "IF", "THEN", "AND", "OR", and "NOT". These eight SRSs were judged to be easy to understand.

165

2) Calculate the relative inter-textual distance among the eight SRSs. LOCAT SRS (one of the eight SRSs) is used as the benchmark SRS (Text A in (Eq.8-5)) because of its size (in terms of the number of tokens). LOCAT SRS is the smallest among these eight SRSs, as required by (Eq.8-5). The average value of the relative inter-textual distance among the eight SRSs is 0.32.

3) Calculate the relative inter-textual distance, $\delta_{(LOCAT,B)}$, between the remaining 40 SRSs and LOCAT's SRS.

4) Judge whether an SRS is easy to understand or not.

5) We found that an SRS is easy to understand in most of the cases when $\delta_{(LOCAT,B)}$ is less than 0.40. An SRS differs from the 8 SRSs in terms of writing style and is difficult to understand in most the cases when $\delta_{(LOCAT,B)}$ is greater than 0.40. Therefore, we decided to use 0.40 as the threshold relative inter-textual distance to classify SRS' writing style into two levels: Style I ($\delta_{(LOCAT,B)} \leq 0.40$) and Style II ($\delta_{(LOCAT,B)} > 0.40$). This decision was also supported by the statistical test results shown in Table 8-2.

The results of the preliminary study for determining the threshold relative inter-textual distance are summarized in Table 8-1.

Table 8-1: Results of the Preliminary Study for Determining the Threshold Relative Inter-textual Distance

SRS index	$\delta_{(LOCAT,B)}$	Easy to Understand?	Assigned Writing Style
SRS-1	0.371	Yes	Style I
SRS-2	0.352	Yes	Style I

166

SRS index	$\delta_{(LOCAT,B)}$	Easy to Understand?	Assigned Writing Style
SRS-3	0.661	No	Style II
SRS-4	0.667	No	Style II
SRS-5	0.546	No	Style II
SRS-6	0.62	No	Style II
SRS-7	0.374	Yes	Style I
SRS-8	0.338	Yes	Style I
SRS-9	0.601	No	Style II
SRS-10	0.435	Yes	Style I
SRS-11	0.560	No	Style II
SRS-12	0.599	No	Style II
SRS-13	0.315	Yes	Style I
SRS-14	0.378	Yes	Style I
SRS-15	0.412	Yes	Style I
SRS-16	0.253	Yes	Style I
SRS-17	0.312	No	Style II
SRS-18	0.334	No	Style II
SRS-19	0.625	No	Style II
SRS-20	0.461	No	Style II
SRS-21	0.348	Yes	Style I
SRS-22	0.487	No	Style II
SRS-23	0.473	No	Style II
SRS-24	0.375	No	Style II
SRS-25	0.335	No	Style II
SRS-26	0.39	Yes	Style I
SRS-27	0.413	No	Style II
SRS-28	0.373	Yes	Style I
SRS-29	0.344	Yes	Style I
SRS-30	0.418	Yes	Style I
SRS-31	0.468	No	Style II
SRS-32	0.382	Yes	Style I
SRS-33	0.352	No	Style II
SRS-34	0.59	No	Style II
SRS-35	0.413	No	Style II

SRS index	$\delta_{(LOCAT,B)}$	Easy to Understand?	Assigned Writing Style
SRS-36	0.342	No	Style II
SRS-37	0.363	Yes	Style I
SRS-38	0.515	Yes	Style I
SRS-39	0.378	Yes	Style I
SRS-40	0.581	No	Style II

Table 8-2 shows the results obtained from statistically testing the population mean of Style I's relative inter-textual distances, $\mu_{\delta_{(LOCAT,Style\,I)}}$, and the population mean of Style II's relative inter-textual distances, $\mu_{\delta_{(LOCAT,Style\,II)}}$, against the selected threshold value (0.4) using the one-sample Student's t-test [102]. According to the results, the accepted hypotheses (at a significant level of 0.05) are $\mu_{\delta_{(LOCAT,Style\,I)}} < 0.4$ for Style I [12] and $\mu_{\delta_{(LOCAT,Style\,II)}} > 0.4$ for Style II[13]. In other words, it is statistically appropriate to use 0.4 as the threshold relative inter-textual distance.

Table 8-2: Results of Testing the Population Mean of Either Style I's or Style's Relative Inter-textual Distances against the Selected Threshold Value ($\alpha = 0.05$)

Population	Size	Degree of freedom	mean	Standard Deviation	t	P-Value
Style I	18	17	0.372	0.0544	-2.197	0.021[14]
Style II	22	21	0.492	0.118	3.632	0.001[15]

---

[12] Null and alternative hypothesis for testing the population mean of Style I's relative inter-textual distances are: H$_o$: $\mu_{\delta_{(LOCAT,Style\,I)}} \geq 0.4$, and H$_a$: $\mu_{\delta_{(LOCAT,Style\,I)}} < 0.4$.

[13] Null and alternative hypothesis for testing the population mean of Style II's relative inter-textual distances are: H$_o$: $\mu_{\delta_{(LOCAT,Style\,II)}} \leq 0.4$, and H$_a$: $\mu_{\delta_{(LOCAT,Style\,II)}} > 0.4$.

[14] This value indicates the odds of $\mu_{\delta_{(LOCAT,Style\,I)}} \geq 0.4$.

[15] This value indicates the odds of $\mu_{\delta_{(LOCAT,Style\,II)}} \leq 0.4$.

It should be noted that the process in which the threshold relative inter-textual distance is determined is somewhat subjective. Further research is required for validating the use of Labbe's Relative Inter-textual Distance as the SRS stylometric characterization.

Definition 8-10: Application Type

The software projects were classified by Jones [103] as six application types. The definitions are given below:

Application Type	Explanation
Commercial software	Applications that are produced for large-scale marketing to hundreds or even millions of clients. Examples of commercial software are Microsoft Word, Excel, etc.
End-user software	Applications written by individuals who are neither professional programmers nor software engineers.
Management information system (MIS)	Applications that enterprises produce in support of their business and administrative operations, such as payroll systems, accounting systems, front- and back-office banking systems, insurance claims handling systems, airline reservation systems, and the like.
Military software	Software produced for a uniformed military service and constrained to follow the standards laid down for this purpose.
Outsourced and contract software	Software produced under a blanket contract by which a software development organization agrees to produce all, or specific categories, of software for the client organization. Contract software is a specific software project that is built under contract for a client organization.
System software (SYSTEM)	Software that controls physical devices. They include the operating systems that control computer hardware, network switching systems, automobile fuel injection systems, and other control systems.

8.2 Research Questions and Hypotheses

This study had a primary major research question and a secondary research question. The primary and secondary research questions were:

1. *Are persons who use the CEC Construction Rules more effective or more efficient in A- CEG construction than persons using the general A-CEG construction guidelines? (Primary research question)*

2. *Do other factors (writing styles of SRS and Type of applications) impact the effectiveness of an inspector? (Secondary research question)*

To our knowledge, these questions have not been previously investigated, and then there are no past findings to be used as hypotheses to be confirmed or rejected.

To investigate these two questions, a more detailed set of six hypotheses were defined. For each hypothesis, the null hypothesis (HX_0) is presented, followed by the alternative hypothesis (HX_a).

$H1_0$ *There is no difference in effectiveness between the subjects applying the A-CEG Construction Rules and the subjects using the general A-CEG construction guideline.*

$H1_a$ *The subjects applying the A-CEG Construction Rules significantly outperform the subjects using the general A-CEG construction guidelines in terms of effectiveness.*

$H2_0$ *There is no difference in efficiency between the subjects applying the A-CEG Construction Rules and the subjects using the general A-CEG construction guideline.*

$H2_a$ *The subjects applying the A-CEG Construction Rules significantly outperform the subjects using the general A-CEG construction guidelines in terms of efficiency.*

$H3_0$ *SRS' writing style does not affect subjects' effectiveness in identifying A-CEG elements.*

$H3_a$ *SRS' writing style significantly affects subjects' effectiveness in identifying A-CEG elements. More specifically, Style I is better than Style*

170

II in terms of effectiveness.

H4o   *SRS' writing style does not affect subjects' efficiency in identifying A-CEG elements.*

H4a   *SRS' writing style significantly affects subjects' efficiency in identifying A-CEG elements. More specifically, Style I is better than Style II in terms of efficiency.*

H5o   *The application type does not affect subjects' effectiveness in identifying A-CEG elements.*

H5a   *The application type significantly affects subjects' effectiveness in identifying A-CEG elements. More specifically, SRSs of type SYSTEM can be handled more effectively than SRSs of type MIS.*

H6o   *The application type does not affect subjects' efficiency in identifying A-CEG elements.*

H6a   *The application type significantly affects subjects' efficiency in identifying A-CEG elements. More specifically, SRSs of type SYSTEM can be handled more efficiently than SRSs of type MIS.*

8.3 *Variables*

Three types of variables were defined for the experiment, *independent, controlled,* and *dependent* variables. Because we did not have enough subjects, we focused our usability test on effectiveness and efficiency, and restricted the target SRSs to be of either SYSTEM or MIS. Moreover, we adopted the Randomized Block Designs techniques [104] to eliminate the experimental error due to nuisance factors. For randomized block designs, there is one factor that is of primary interest and several other nuisance factors that may affect the measured result, but are not of primary interest. The primary factor for this experiment was the A-CEG construction method used. The nuisance factors were the SRS' writing style and the SRS' application type.

8.3.1 Independent Variables

Experiment D manipulated three independent variables:

o the A-CEG construction method used. The experiment groups used either the general A-CEG construction guidelines (excerpted from [45 pp. 65-88], for Group I), or the A-CEG Construction Rules (for Group II).

o the SRS' writing style, with two values: Style I ($\delta_{(LOCAT,B)} \leq 0.40$) and Style II ($\delta_{(LOCAT,B)} > 0.40$).

o the SRS' application type, with two values: MIS and SYSTEM.

8.3.2 Controlled Variables

The controlled variables were

o Standard that an SRS complies with: one level (all preselected SRSs follow IEEE Std. 830-1998 [53]).

o Size of SRSs (SRS' size is measured in terms of number of sentences): one level (small)

o Educational Background (field in which a subject's advanced degrees were awarded): one level (all subjects' educational background is non computer-related).

o Industrial experience: one level (all subjects have no industrial experience on software development)

172

8.3.3 Dependent Variables

Experiment D measured the following dependent variables:

o Time to learn, measured in minutes (T_1)

o Time spent on finding A-CEG elements, measured in minutes (T_2)

o Number of true positives (TPs)

o Number of true negatives (TNs)

o Number of false positives (FPs)

o Number of false negatives (FNs)

o Accuracy, measured as: $Accuracy = \dfrac{TPs + TNs}{TPs + FPs + TNs + FNs}$

o Recall, measured as: $Recall = \dfrac{TPs}{TPs + FNs}$

o Precision, measured as: $Precision = \dfrac{TPs}{TPs + FPs}$

o Efficiency, measured as: $Efficiency = \dfrac{TPs + TNs}{T_2}$

Among these dependent variables, the first six were direct measures. The last four were indirect measures and were calculated using the direct measures.

8.4 Subjects

The subjects were four PhD students of a graduate level course on Software Quality Analysis at the University of Maryland. The experiment was performed as a 13-week term class project mandatory for the course, ensuring the necessary motivation. The experiment served the educational objective of teaching students a black-box test cases design technique, as required by the course curriculum.

173

The subjects neither were notified about the experiment nor knew what the experimental variables were to ensure that they would not be influenced by the knowledge of the experiment. Preventive steps were taken to ensure that the students had no unwanted communications during the course.

8.5 Experiment Materials

The experiment materials were:

- IEEE standard IEEE Std. 830-1998 [53]
- Eighteen SRS segments adapted from the functional requirements sections of ten preselected SRSs
- General experiment instructions
- The general A-CEG construction guidelines used in industry (excerpted from [45 pp. 65-88], for Group I only)
- The A-CEG Construction Rules (for Group II only)
- CEG report forms and time log-sheets (shown in Appendix E)
- A questionnaire to assess subjects' background (shown in Appendix F)
- A questionnaire to assess the ease of use of the A-CEG construction Rules (shown in Appendix G)

All preselected SRSs were written in plain text English natural language and adhered to the IEEE specification standard IEEE Std. 830-1998 [53]. The SRSs were analyzed for defects prior to the experiment by an independent inspector (the author). This was necessary because the requirements were assumed to be correct for the purpose of the experiment. These SRSs were the requirements documents for the following systems:

1. CHAIRMAN Conference Management System (CCMS) [105]: a web application that supports every aspect of the conference organization process. This includes paper submission, reviewer assignments, revised and camera-ready paper submission, registration handling of the conference participants.

2. Invisible Meeting Scheduler (IMS) [106]: a software application to assist in the scheduling of meetings among individuals whose schedules are available in an online calendar.

3. LOCAT [63]: a real-time simple projectile tracking system for the Army's all weather Doppler radar system called TRAC. The software is part of a host software subsystem called COMP running on a Sparc 4 system at 0.08 MIPS.

4. PACS [88]: a personal access control system.

5. Student Registry Query System (SRQS) [107]: an application designed for students to create and manage their accounts online. Registry DB is a database that maintains student SSN, student login ID, student password, course information, and registration information.

6. Search PUBS (SSP) [108]: an application designed for generating queries in order to interact with the PUBS database. PUBS is a database consisting of information on authors listing fields of last name, first name, publications and the city, which they belong to.

7. SXXX [40]: a part of a digital protection system used in nuclear power plants.

8. Tellerfast [109]: a software package performing as a part of the Automated Teller Machine (ATM) system described in the system requirements specifications of the Bank of HESUS. This software product provides the control necessary for the ATM system to perform its activities.

9. The Energy Management System (THEMAS) [110]: an energy management system that operates independent of any other system, or any components of the heating and cooling system to which it is attached.

10. Word Processor Unit (WPU) [111]: an application designed to perform word processing using functions such as adding text, deleting text, word and character counting based on the user input.

Each SRS segment used in Experiment D contained a complete set of sections for a functional module, including "Input Section", "Processing Section", and "Output Section". Table 8-3 presents some basic information for the SRS segments used in the experiment.

Table 8-3: Basic Information on SRS Segments Used in Experiment D

Index of SRS Segment	SRS	Writing Style	Application Type	Experiment Phase in which the SRS segment was used
S-Training1	LOCAT	Style I	SYSTEM	Phase I (Preparation and Training)
S-Training2	Tellerfast	Style II	MIS	
S1	SRQS	Style I	MIS	Phase II (Implementation)
S2				
S3	SSP	Style I	MIS	
S4				
S5	PACS	Style I	SYSTEM	
S6				
S7	WPU	Style I	SYSTEM	

S8				
S9 / S10	CCMS	Style II	MIS	
S11 / S12	IMS	Style II	MIS	
S13 / S14	SXXX	Style II	SYSTEM	
S15 / S16	THEMAS	Style II	SYSTEM	

In addition, the SRS segments used in Phase II (S1 to S16) were thoroughly examined and a list of causes, effects, constraints, and logical relationships was produced. This list was prepared by an individual (the author) who was very familiar with the applications and the CEGA techniques. The aggregation numbers for this list are shown in Table 8-4.

Table 8-4: Data on SRS Segments Used in Experiment Phase II

Index of SRS segment	Size of SRS segment		Number of				Total number of A-CEG elements
	Number of pages	Number of sentences	Causes	Effects	Constraints	Logical relationships[16]	
S1	3	35	11	8	6	19	44
S2	3	34	8	9	5	18	40
S3	3	33	8	9	4	19	40
S4	3	32	7	11	5	22	45
S5	3	37	9	7	6	17	39
S6	3	31	8	9	5	20	42

---

[16] The number of logical relationships was counted in terms of the four basic logical relationships: "IDENTITY", "AND", "OR", and "NOT".

Index of SRS segment	Size of SRS segment		Number of				Total number of A-CEG elements
	Number of pages	Number of sentences	Causes	Effects	Constraints	Logical relationships[16]	
S7	3	34	8	10	5	21	44
S8	3	36	10	6	5	18	39
S9	3	32	11	8	6	19	44
S10	3	34	9	9	5	18	41
S11	3	35	10	9	5	20	44
S12	3	32	8	11	5	20	44
S13	3	36	10	7	6	16	39
S14	3	35	9	9	4	20	42
S15	3	34	10	8	6	17	41
S16	3	36	8	11	3	23	45

8.6 Procedure

The experiment consists of two phases: Training and Preparation (Phase I), and Implementation (Phase II).

During Phase I, all subjects were prepared with a set of training lectures on IEEE standard for SRS and A-CEG construction. Apart from the theory presentations, the sessions consisted of an in-class questionnaire and an in-class quiz, and practical demonstrations of the techniques. Care was taken to avoid any biases that were suspected to be present.

During Phase II, all subjects were given four sets of assignment packages to complete the experimental tasks.

8.6.1 Training and Preparation (Phase I)

The first phase of the experiment lasted three weeks.

178

The subjects were first given a questionnaire with ten questions to appraise their knowledge on CEGA, requirements analysis, and industry experience. The questionnaire showed that students had same type of backgrounds. Therefore, it was not necessary to take effort to mitigate the effect of the background factor from the experiment.

We then gave a 1.5-hour lecture on the IEEE standard for SRS and taught A-CEG construction. A sample SRS (S-Training1 in Table 8-3) was presented and an assignment was given for finding A-CEG elements. The results were discussed in class and a list of known A-CEG elements was written out according to the schema of A-CEG elements report forms. We then introduced a new SRS (S-Training2 in Table 8-3). As an in-class quiz, students were asked to individually read the SRS and record A-CEG elements on the CEG report forms to be used in this experiment. Subjects took the quiz in a classroom with enough space to avoid plagiarism. After the quiz, we discussed with students the list of known A-CEG elements and what A-CEG elements that they had actually found.

The subjects were then ordered by expected performance and randomly assigned to the two groups (Group I and Group II) in such a manner that one out of any two subjects with similar expected performance would be assigned to each group. This step was taken to avoid bias. Since no better information was available, we used the scores from the quiz assignments for estimating the subjects' expected performance. We do not claim that this arrangement provides perfect matches, but other studies found that this usually results in groups with reasonably balanced average subject ability.

179

Another two lectures were given to Group I and Group II, separately. Subjects in Group I were instructed how to use the general A-CEG construction guidelines while subjects in Group II were instructed how to use the A-CEG Construction Rules. Each lecture lasted 2-hour long.

Finally, all subjects were given a lecture on the whole process of Phase II experiment, explaining the goals and the specific process to be used in the experiment. In addition, the students were instructed to work independently and record every event. The students were also given log-sheets and were demonstrated how to use them. The experiment details were recorded on log-sheets. The students recorded the time taken, nature and the possible cause of any events in the log-sheets. There were extra credits for using log-sheets which provided them the necessary motivation. While designing the log-sheet, it was ensured that it is very easy to fill in and that it is not ambiguous. This ensured that the extra burden on the subjects because of the log-sheets was minimal.

Questions were encouraged during the class but no interactions were allowed among students outside the class. Students were strictly instructed to avoid outside-class communications. We were always present to answer questions and preventing unwanted communication. All questions to the instructor, outside the class were through help sessions. Events in lecture and the help sessions were recorded for the learning time measure.

8.6.2 Running the Experiment (Phase II)

After the last lecture, all students were assigned four assignment packages. This part of the experiment lasted 8 weeks/2 months.

180

Each assignment package contained:

1. instructions for the assigned task

2. an SRS segment

3. either the general A-CEG construction guidelines (for Group I) or the A-CEG
   Construction Rules set (for Group II)

4. blank CEG report forms

5. a log-sheet for A-CEG elements finding time

The instructions for the students were:

1. The assignment is due in two weeks.

2. No communication with other students in regard to the assignment is allowed.

3. The textual requirements are assumed to be correct.

4. Read through all documents briefly before starting to work.

5. The main task is to identify and record A-CEG elements (including causes,
   effects, logical relationships, and constraints) in the assigned SRS segment.

6. Log all clock times about the activities.

7. When finished, verify that the logged data seem to be correct and hand them
   in.

The four assignment packages were assigned one after another rather than being
assigned all at once. The next package was assigned when the previous package was
submitted. After each student turned in the assignments and log-sheets, the data was
briefly examined for errors and missing information in the record in order to get as

accurate data as possible. **Error! Reference source not found.** shows the assignment

information on the SRS segments.

Table 8-5: Assignments of SRS Segments

SRS Segment Index	SRS	Writing Style	Type of Application	Student Assigned	Group Assigned
S1	SRQS	Style I	MIS	Student A	Group I
S2				Student B	Group II
S3	SSP	Style I	MIS	Student C	Group I
S4				Student D	Group II
S5	PACS	Style I	SYSTEM	Student A	Group I
S6				Student B	Group II
S7	LOCAT	Style I	SYSTEM	Student C	Group I
S8				Student D	Group II
S9	CCMS	Style II	MIS	Student A	Group I
S10				Student B	Group II
S11	IMS	Style II	MIS	Student C	Group I
S12				Student D	Group II
S13	SXXX	Style II	SYSTEM	Student A	Group I
S14				Student B	Group II
S15	THEMAS	Style II	SYSTEM	Student C	Group I
S16				Student D	Group II

A postmortem questionnaire (see Appendix G) with nine questions was sent to the

students at the end of the experiment to assess the subjective measures of usability,

satisfaction and ease, and to help us understand the opinion of the participants toward

the A-CEG technique.

The entire design for Experiment D is provided in Table 8-6.

Table 8-6: Entire Design of Experiment D

Group	Activity									
I	Q_1	T_1	Q_2	M_1	R	T_{2-1}	M_{2-1}	S	Q_3	M_3
II						T_{2-2}	M_{2-2}			

Where

Q_1 : Delivering and collecting a questionnaire to distinguish subjects' background of knowledge and industry experience.

T_1 : Training all subjects on IEEE standard IEEE Std. 830-1998 for SRS and A-CEG construction (1.5 hours)

Q_2 : Assigning a quiz to distinguish student's expected performance of A-CEG construction (0.5 hours)

M_1 : Measuring the students' expected performance.

R : Randomization according to subjects' expected performance

T_{2-1} : Training Group I on using the general A-CEG construction guidelines (2 hours)

T_{2-2} : Training Group II on using the A-CEG Construction Rules (2 hours)

M_{2-1} : Measuring time that Group I students need to master the guidelines.

M_{2-2} : Measuring time that Group II students need to master the A-CEG Construction Rules.

S : SRS assignments (12 weeks)

Q_3 : Delivering and collecting a postmortem questionnaire asking for subjective judgments on the usability, satisfaction and ease of the A-CEG construction method. (0.5 hours)

M_3 : Measuring subjects' performance and analyzing results

183

8.7 *Experiment Results and Discussion*

Table 8-7 presents the experiment data used in statistical tests.

Table 8-7: Experiment Data Used for Hypotheses Testing

SRS Segment Index	Independent Variable			Dependent Variable				
	A-CEG Construction Method	Writing Style	Type of Application	TP	TN	FP	FN	T_2, minutes
S1	Group I	Style I	MIS	37	0	0	7	84.5
S2	Group II	Style I	MIS	34	0	2	6	75.5
S3	Group I	Style I	MIS	33	0	1	7	83
S4	Group II	Style I	MIS	40	0	1	5	76
S5	Group I	Style I	SYSTEM	32	0	1	7	87
S6	Group II	Style I	SYSTEM	38	0	2	4	77.5
S7	Group I	Style I	SYSTEM	36	0	2	8	85
S8	Group II	Style I	SYSTEM	33	0	1	6	81.5
S9	Group I	Style II	MIS	33	0	3	11	84.5
S10	Group II	Style II	MIS	34	0	2	7	85
S11	Group I	Style II	MIS	32	0	2	12	87.5
S12	Group II	Style II	MIS	36	0	3	8	91.5
S13	Group I	Style II	SYSTEM	28	0	3	11	95
S14	Group II	Style II	SYSTEM	35	0	2	7	89.5
S15	Group I	Style II	SYSTEM	28	0	2	13	85
S16	Group II	Style II	SYSTEM	32	0	3	13	90

8.7.1 Statistical Analysis

In this section, we focus on descriptive analysis and statistical tests for proposed hypotheses. All hypotheses are analyzed taking the following steps:

Step 1: Calculating the descriptive statistical data. These data are then displayed using a box plot for the comparison analysis of the commonalities and differences between two populations. A *box plot* (also known as a box-and-whisker diagram) is a convenient way of graphically depicting groups of numerical data through five-number summaries, including minimum, 25% quartile, median, 75% quartile, and maximum [102].

Step 2: Performing one-tailed F-test (two-sample for variances). The *F-test* is used to test for differences among sample variance [102]. This test can be a two-tailed test or a one-tailed test. The two-tailed version tests against the alternative hypothesis that the standard deviations are not equal. The one-tailed version only tests the standard deviation from the first population is either greater than or less than (but not both) the second population standard deviation.

Step 3: Performing two-sample Student's t-test. *Student's t-test* is one of the most commonly used techniques for testing a hypothesis on the basis of a difference between sample means for small samples, usually less than thirty [102]. It is applied when the population is assumed to be normally distributed but the sample sizes are small enough that the statistic on which inference is based is not normally distributed because it relies on an uncertain estimate of standard deviation rather than on a precisely known value [102].

Step 4: Performing Mann–Whitney U test (also called Wilcoxon rank-sum test, or Wilcoxon-Mann-Whitney test). The *Mann-Whitney U test* is a non-parametric alternative to the two-sample Student's t-test when the population

185

cannot be assumed to be normally distributed [102]. In Experiment D, we use the Mann-Whitney U test as a subsidiary to the Student's t-test.

Step 5: Drawing a conclusion about the hypothesis test by either accepting the null hypothesis or rejecting the null in favor of the alternative hypothesis. The significance value of rejecting the null hypotheses is 0.05 for all tests.

8.7.1.1. Impact of A-CEG Construction Method on Effectiveness (Hypothesis H1)

Table 8-8 presents the descriptive statistics for the impact of the A-CEG Construction method (independent variable) on the effectiveness (dependent variable). This independent variable was defined with two levels: either using the general A-CEG construction guidelines (Group I) or using the A-CEG Construction Rules set (Group II).

Table 8-8: Descriptive Statistics for the Impact of A-CEG Construction Method on Effectiveness

A-CEG Construction Method	Dependent Variable	Mean	Standard Deviation	Min	Lower Quart	Median	Upper Quart	Max
Group I	Accuracy, %	74.3	7.07	65.1	68.9	74.2	80.1	84.1
	Recall, %	77.29	6.03	68.3	72.5	78.4	82.2	84.1
	Precision, %	94.8	3.20	90	92.8	94.5	97.0	100.0
Group II	Accuracy, %	80.1	5.80	68.8	78.5	80.3	83.5	87.0
	Recall, %	83.5	5.84	71.1	82.6	84.0	86.0	90.5
	Precision, %	94.9	1.89	92	94	94.5	95.5	98

The box plots in Figure 8-2 graphically show the impact of the A-CEG construction method on the effectiveness.

186

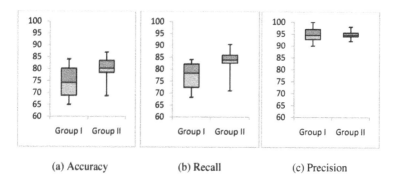

(a) Accuracy   (b) Recall   (c) Precision

Figure 8-2: Impact of A-CEG construction method on the Effectiveness

Table 8-9 presents the results obtained from the F-test, Student's t-test, and Mann-Whitney U test using SPSS Statistics® [112]. In this table, "N" represents observations, "df" short for "degree of freedom", and "t-Stat" for "t-Statistic".

Table 8-9: Statistical Testing Results for Hypothesis H1 ($\alpha = 0.05$)

Independent Variable	Dependent Variable	N	F-test			Student's t-test			Mann-Whitney U test
			df	F	P(F<=f) 1-tailed	df	t-Stat	P(T<=t) 1-tailed[17]	P-value 1-tailed
A-CEG Construction Method	Accuracy	8	7	1.55	0.289	14	-1.77	0.049	0.0805
	Recall	8	7	1.07	0.468	14	-2.10	0.027	0.019
	Precision	8	7	3.50	0.060	14	-0.16	0.438	0.323

<hr />

[17] The value of "P(T <= t) 1-tailed" indicates the False Negative Rate β, the probability of failing to reject a null hypothesis. $1 - \beta$ is the power of a test.

The results of F-tests ($P(F \leq f) = 0.289$, $P(F \leq f) = 0.468$, and $P(F \leq f) = 0.060$) indicate that there is no significant difference in variances between samples for the accuracy, recall, and precision measure, respectively.

The results of both Student's t-test ($P(T \leq t) = 0.438$) and Mann-Whitney U test ($P = 0.323$) show that there is no significant effect of the A-CEG construction method on the precision at $\alpha = 0.05$. However, a main effect of the A-CEG construction method on accuracy and recall was observed ($P(T \leq t) = 0.049$, $P = 0.0805$ for accuracy, and $P(T \leq t) = 0.027$, $P = 0.019$ for recall), suggesting that Group II (using the A-CEG construction rules set) produced more accurate CEG elements, and missed less CEG elements than Group I. These allow $H1_0$ to be rejected in favor of $H1_a$.

8.7.1.2. Impact of A-CEG Construction Method on Efficiency (Hypothesis H2)

Table 8-10 follows the presentation style used in Table 8-8, but deals with efficiency instead of effectiveness.

Table 8-10: Descriptive statistics for the Impact of A-CEG Construction Method on Efficiency

A-CEG Construction Method	Dependent Variable	Mean	Standard Deviation	Min	Lower Quart	Median	Upper Quart	Max
Group I	Efficiency, A-CEG elements/hr	22.6	2.84	17.7	21.4	22.8	24.8	26.3
Group II		25.6	3.45	21.3	23.6	24.2	27.6	31.6

The box plot in Figure 8-3 graphically shows the impact of the A-CEG construction method on the efficiency.

188

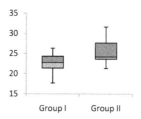

Figure 8-3: Impact of A-CEG Construction Method on Efficiency

Table 8-11 presents the results obtained from the F-test, Student's t-test, and Mann-Whitney U test using SPSS Statistics® [112]. In this table, "N" represents observations, "df" short for "degree of freedom", and "t-Stat" for "t-Statistic".

Table 8-11: Statistical Testing Results for Hypothesis H2 ($\alpha = 0.05$)

Independent Variable	Dependent Variable	N	F-test			Student's t-test			Mann-Whitney U test
			df	F	P(F<=f) 1-tailed	df	t-Stat	P(T<=t) 1-tailed[18]	P-value 1-tailed
A-CEG Construction Method	Efficiency	8	7	0.68	0.309	14	-1.91	0.038	0.0525

The results of the F-test ($P(F \le f) = 0.309$) indicate that there is no significant difference in variances between samples for the efficiency measure.

The results of both Student's t-test ($P(T \le t) = 0.038$) and Mann-Whitney U test ($P = 0.0525$) show that there is a significant effect of the A-CEG construction

---

[18] The value of "P(T <= t) 1-tailed" indicates the False Negative Rate β, the probability of failing to reject a null hypothesis. $1 - \beta$ is the power of a test.

method on the efficiency at $\alpha = 0.05$, suggesting that Group II (using the A-CEG construction rules set) were more efficient in identifying CEG elements. These allow H2$_0$ to be rejected in favor of H2$_a$.

8.7.1.3. Impact of SRS' Writing Style on Effectiveness (Hypothesis H3)

Table 8-12 presents the descriptive statistics for the impact of the SRS' writing style (independent variable) on the effectiveness (dependent variable). This independent variable was defined with two levels: Style I and Style II.

Table 8-12: Descriptive Statistics for the Impact of SRS' Writing Styles on Effectiveness

SRS' Writing Style	Dependent Variable	Mean	Standard Deviation	Min	Lower Quart	Median	Upper Quart	Max
Style I	Accuracy, %	82.4	3.16	78.3	80.4	81.8	84.7	87.0
	Recall, %	84.9	3.19	81.8	82.4	84.4	86.0	90.5
	Precision, %	96.6	1.93	94.0	94.9	97.1	97.2	100.0
Style II	Accuracy, %	71.9	5.91	65.1	66.7	69.9	77.2	79.5
	Recall, %	75.9	5.94	68.3	71.6	73.9	82.1	83.3
	Precision, %	92.8	1.58	90.3	91.6	92.8	94.2	94.6

The box plots in Figure 8-4 graphically show the impact of the SRS' writing style on the effectiveness.

190

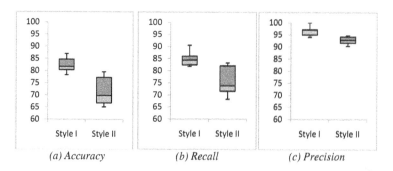

(a) Accuracy   (b) Recall   (c) Precision

Figure 8-4: Impact of Writing Style on Effectiveness

Table 8-13 presents the results obtained from the F-test, Student's t-test, and

Mann-Whitney U test using SPSS Statistics® [112]. In this table, "N" represents

observations, "df" short for "degree of freedom", and "t-Stat" for "t-Statistic".

Table 8-13: Statistical Testing Results for Hypothesis H3 ($\alpha = 0.05$)

Independent Variable	Dependent Variable	N	F-test			Student's t-test			Mann-Whitney U test
			df	F	P(F<=f) 1-tailed	df	t-Stat	P(T<=t) 1-tailed[19]	P-value 1-tailed
SRS' Writing Style	Accuracy	8	7	0.28	0.059	14	4.60	0.00021	0.0005
	Recall	8	7	0.29	0.060	14	3.81	0.00097	0.0025
	Precision	8	7	1.5	0.302	14	4.31	0.00036	0.0005

---

[19] The value of "P(T <= t) 1-tailed" indicates the False Negative Rate β, the probability of failing to reject a null hypothesis. $1 - \beta$ is the power of a test.

The results of F-tests ($P(F \leq f) = 0.059$, $P(F \leq f) = 0.060$, and $P(F \leq f) = 0.302$) indicate that there is no significant difference in variances between samples for the accuracy, recall, and precision measure, respectively.

The results of both Student's t-test ($P(T \leq t) = 0.00021$, $P(T \leq t) = 0.00097$, and $P(T \leq t) = 0.00036$) and Mann-Whitney U test ($P = 0.0005$, $P = 0.0025$, and $P = 0.005$) show that there are strongly significant effects of the SRS' writing style on the accuracy, recall, and precision at $\alpha = 0.05$, suggesting that A-CEG elements in SRSs of Style I were identified more effectively than those in SRSs of Style II. These allow H3_0 to be rejected in favor of H3_a.

8.7.1.4. Impact of SRS' Writing Style on Efficiency (Hypothesis H4)

Table 8-14 follows the presentation style used in Table 8-12, but deals with efficiency instead of effectiveness.

Table 8-14: Descriptive Statistics for the Impact of SRS' Writing Style on Efficiency

SRS' Writing Style	Dependent Variable	Mean	Standard Deviation	Min	Lower Quart	Median	Upper Quart	Max
Style I	Efficiency, A-CEG elements/hr	26.25	3.08	22.1	24.2	25.9	27.6	31.6
Style II		21.9	2.22	17.7	21.0	22.7	23.5	24.0

The box plot in Figure 8-5 graphically shows the impact of the SRS' writing style on the efficiency.

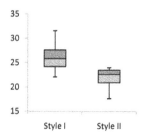

Figure 8-5: Impact of Writing Style on Efficiency

Table 8-15 presents the results obtained from the F-test, Student's t-test, and Mann-Whitney U test using SPSS Statistics® [112]. In this table, "N" represents observations, "df" short for "degree of freedom", and "t-Stat" for "t-Statistic".

Table 8-15: Statistical Testing Results for Hypothesis H4 ($\alpha = 0.05$)

Independent Variable	Dependent Variable	N	F-test			Student's t-test			Mann-Whitney U test
			df	F	P(F<=f) 1-tailed	df	t-Stat	P(T<=t) 1-tailed[20]	P-value 1-tailed
SRS' Writing Style	Efficiency	8	7	1.92	0.204	14	3.24	0.00296	0.0015

The results of the F-test ($P(F \leq f) = 0.204$) indicate that there is no significant difference in variances between samples for the efficiency measure.

The results of both Student's t-test ($P(T \leq t) = 0.00296$) and Mann-Whitney U test ($P = 0.0015$) show that there is a strongly significant effect of the SRS' writing style

---

[20] The value of "P(T <=t) 1-tailed" indicates the False Negative Rate β, the probability of failing to reject a null hypothesis. $1 - \beta$ is the power of a test.

on the efficiency at $\alpha = 0.05$, suggesting that A-CEG elements in SRSs of Style I were identified more efficiently than those in SRSs of Style II. These allow $H4_0$ to be rejected in favor of $H4_a$.

8.7.1.5. Impact of SRS' Application Type on Effectiveness (Hypothesis H5)

Table 8-16 presents the descriptive statistics for the impact of the SRS' application type (independent variable) on the effectiveness (dependent variable). This independent variable was defined with two levels: SYSTEM and MIS.

Table 8-16: Descriptive Statistics for the Impact of SRS' Application Type on Effectiveness

SRS' Writing Style	Dependent Variable	Mean	Standard Deviation	Min	Lower Quart	Median	Upper Quart	Max
SYSTEM	Accuracy, %	78.4	6.67	66.7	76.9	79.8	81.8	86.4
	Recall, %	81.8	5.87	71.8	80.3	83.1	84.3	90.5
	Precision, %	94.7	2.98	90.3	93.7	94.5	95.5	100.0
MIS	Accuracy, %	76.3	7.32	65.1	70.5	77.45	81	87
	Recall, %	79.0	7.31	68.3	72.3	81.8	83.0	88.9
	Precision, %	95.4	2.06	92.3	93.9	95.9	97.1	97.6

The box plots in Figure 8-6 graphically show the impact of the SRS' application type on the effectiveness.

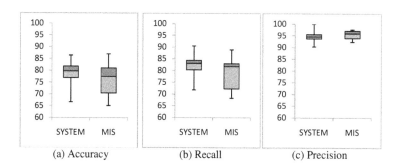

(a) Accuracy (b) Recall (c) Precision

Figure 8-6: Impact of Application Type on Effectiveness

Table 8-17 presents the results obtained from the F-test, Student's t-test, and Mann-Whitney U test using SPSS Statistics® [112]. In this table, "N" represents observations, "df" short for "degree of freedom", and "t-Stat" for "t-Statistic".

Table 8-17: Statistical Testing Results for Hypothesis H5 ($\alpha = 0.05$)

Independent Variable	Dependent Variable	N	F-test			Student's t-test			Mann-Whitney U test
			df	F	P(F<=f) 1-tailed	df	t-Stat	P(T<=t) 1-tailed[21]	P-value 1-tailed
SRS' Application Type	Accuracy	8	7	0.83	0.406	14	0.59	0.281	0.287
	Recall	8	7	0.64	0.288	14	0.87	0.200	0.140
	Precision	8	7	2.09	0.176	14	-0.58	0.574	0.253

---

[21] The value of "P(T <= t) 1-tailed" indicates the False Negative Rate β, the probability of failing to reject a null hypothesis. 1 − β is the power of a test.

The results of F-tests ($P(F \leq f) = 0.406$, $P(F \leq f) = 0.288$, and $P(F \leq f) = 0.176$) indicate that there is no significant difference in variances between samples for the accuracy, recall, and precision measure, respectively.

The results of both Student's t-test ($P(T \leq t) = 0.281$, $P(T \leq t) = 0.200$, and $P(T \leq t) = 0.574$) and Mann-Whitney U test ($P = 0.287$, $P = 0.140$, and $P = 0.253$) show that there are no significant effects of the SRS' application type on the accuracy, recall, and precision at $\alpha = 0.05$. These allow H5_0 to be accepted.

8.7.1.6. Impact of SRS' Application Type on Efficiency (Hypothesis H6)

Table 8-18 follows the presentation style used in Table 8-16, but deals with efficiency instead of effectiveness.

Table 8-18: Descriptive Statistics for the Impact of SRS' Application Type on Efficiency

SRS' Application Type	Dependent Variable	Mean	Standard Deviation	Min	Lower Quart	Median	Upper Quart	Max
SYSTEM	Efficiency, A-CEG elements/hr	24.2	3.53	17.7	23.1	23.8	26.5	29.4
MIS		24.0	3.57	19.8	21.8	23.8	24.6	31.6

The box plot in Figure 8-7 graphically shows the impact of the SRS' application type on the efficiency.

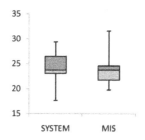

Figure 8-7: Impact of Application Type on Efficiency

Table 8-19 presents the results obtained from the F-test, Student's t-test, and Mann-Whitney U test using SPSS Statistics® [112]. In this table, "N" represents observations, "df" short for "degree of freedom", and "t-Stat" for "t-Statistic".

Table 8-19: Statistical Testing Results for Hypothesis H6 ($\alpha = 0.05$)

Independent Variable	Dependent Variable	N	F-test			Student's t-test			Mann-Whitney U test
			df	F	P(F<=f) 1-tailed	df	t-Stat	P(T<=t) 1-tailed[22]	P-value 1-tailed
SRS' Application Type	Efficiency	8	7	0.98	0.487	14	0.11	0.456	0.399

The results of the F-test ($P(F \leq f) = 0.487$) indicate that there is no significant difference in variances between samples for the efficiency measure.

---

[22] The value of "P(T <= t) 1-tailed" indicates the False Negative Rate β, the probability of failing to reject a null hypothesis. $1 - \beta$ is the power of a test.

197

The results of both Student's t-test ($P(T \leq t) = 0.456$) and Mann-Whitney U test ($P = 0.399$) show that there is no significant effect of the SRS' application type on the efficiency at $\alpha = 0.05$. These allow H6$_0$ to be accepted.

8.7.2 Summary of Statistical Testing

Table 8-20 provides the summary of the statistical tests. Overall, the statistical testing results indicate two things:

1. The A-CEG Construction Rules are helpful in identifying A-CEG elements. Subjects using the A-CEG Construction Rules committed false positives and false negatives less frequently and identified the true positives more efficiently.

2. The SRS' writing style has a significant impact on the identification of A-CEG elements. SRSs of Style I were handled far more effectively and efficiently than SRSs of Style II.

The most surprising finding is that the application type, which was assumed important, was shown to have no statistically significant impact on A-CEG construction. Note that this conclusion was drawn on the basis of the comparison between SYSTEM and MIS. It may not be true for the comparison among other application types.

Table 8-20: Summary of Statistical Tests

Hypothesis	Testing Result	Explanation
H1	Accepted $H1_a$	The subjects applying the A-CEG Construction Rules significantly outperform the subjects using the general A-CEG construction guidelines in terms of effectiveness.
H2	Accepted $H2_a$	The subjects applying the A-CEG Construction Rules significantly outperform the subjects using the general A-CEG construction guidelines in terms of efficiency.
H3	Accepted $H3_a$	SRS' writing style significantly affects subjects' effectiveness in identifying A-CEG elements.
H4	Accepted $H4_a$	SRS' writing style significantly affects subjects' efficiency in identifying A-CEG elements.
H5	Accepted $H5_0$	The impact of SRS' application type on subjects' effectiveness in identifying A-CEG elements is relatively small and not statistically significant
H6	Accepted $H6_0$	The impact of SRS' application type on subjects' efficiency in identifying A-CEG elements is relatively small and not statistically significant

8.7.3 Qualitative Analysis

Table 8-7 presents the experiment data used for qualitative analysis. A major caveat would be that the postmortem questionnaire (see Appendix G) measured subjects' stated opinions rather than their actual ones, which could be markedly at odds with this.

Table 8-21: Experiment data for Qualitative Analysis

Subject	Group	T_1, minutes	Answers to Postmortem Questionnaire				
			Q1 (Usefulness) [23]	Q2 (Ease of use) [24]	Q3 (Ease of Learning) [25]	Q4 (Satisfaction) [26]	Q5 (In general) [27]

[23] For this column, the answer with "1" represents the most useful and "5" the least useful.
[24] For this column, the answer with "1" represents the easiest and "5" the most difficult.
[25] For this column, the answer with "1" represents the easiest and "5" the most difficult.
[26] For this column, the answer with "1" represents the most satisfactory and "5" the least satisfactory.
[27] For this column, the answer with "1" represents the best and "5" the worst.

Subject	Group	T_1, minutes	Answers to Postmortem Questionnaire				
			Q1 (Usefulness)[23]	Q2 (Ease of use)[24]	Q3 (Ease of Learning)[25]	Q4 (Satisfaction)[26]	Q5 (In general)[27]
Student A	I	285	1	4	3	4	3
Student C	I	293	2	4	3	2	2
Student B	II	302	2	4	3	4	3
Student D	II	291	2	2	1	2	2

- Learning Time (T_1)

According to Table 8-21, all subjects spent almost the same amount of learning time. This is partly because most of the learning time was spent in in-class trainings, which was equal by design. The only differences among the subjects were the times spent in help sessions. However, the differences between the subject/groups are small.

- User Satisfaction

There is no significant difference in user satisfaction between two groups. In general, subjects of both groups were not very satisfied with either of the A-CEG construction methods. This indicates the need to improve the A-CEG Construction Rules in terms of the ease of use and ease of learning.

- Excerpted Comments from Subjects

Student A: "... It is hard to distinguish between causes and effects just based on the SRS. This is maybe due to the fact that there is not enough information in SRS itself, or the SRS itself is vague. ..."

Student B: "... The CEG is useful in the sense that it gives a good picture of the SRS and how it is organized. Moreover, graphical representations are usually a good

200

way to picture how things work. But the difference between cause and effect is still

not clear. I believe the method of filling in tables could be a good way to work

with. ..."

Student C: *"... I like the fact that there are a low number of different elements*

and operations for the CEG. This small variety helped me to quickly understand the

notation and the basic rules to design a CEG. Moreover, it offers a clean overview of

the specifications which is important to better spot defects. On the other hand, I found

that the definitions of cause and effect were not properly stated. It took me some time

to figure out that cause indicates everything external, related to the user, and effect

includes both consequences and actions. Maybe a better definition of effect could

help novice users to quickly understand the potential of CEG. ..."

Student D: *"... The rules help in understanding how to construct the CEG and*

how to handle the duplications. However, the use of action words in finding events is

not practical because many events were not related to any action words. ..."

8.8 *Threats to Validity*

As with any empirical study, there are various threats to validity that must be discussed. This section explains the major threats to validity in this study.

The first threat is the threat of a selection bias in the subject population. The specific subjects who participated in this study could be the major source of the observed result and may not be repeatable by other researchers. This threat was alleviated to some degree by the fact that the participants were selected without any prior information about the composition of the class or participants. In addition, the participants did not receive any compensation for participation in the study. They all participated as a part of their class project and therefore the level of motivation of each subject should have been similar.

The second threat, the representativeness of the artifact is a threat to external validity. It is possible that the SRSs used in this study may not be reflective of an actual requirements document. This threat is addressed to some degree by the fact that the SRSs were selected from public academia and industry projects. Hence these SRSs describe a realistic piece of software that is not a trivial system.

The third thread is the experience of subjects' - the most frequent concern with experiments using student subjects is that the results cannot be generalized to professionals. Experience is certainly an issue for this experiment, where the subjects had no industrial experience. However, we do not believe that the experiment was influenced by our subjects' limited experience with SRS analysis, because implementing A-CEG construction was rather straightforward.

The last threat is one that is common to any empirical study. Researchers cannot draw a general conclusion based solely on the results of one study. Because of the presence of a large number of context variables, both known and unknown to the researchers, it cannot be assumed that results will always generalize beyond the setting in which the study was conducted. More confidence in a result comes from replication of a study. Therefore, this study needs to be replicated to build a body of empirical knowledge to allow concrete, general conclusions to be drawn.

8.9 Summary

The objective of Experiment D is to compare and hence evaluate how well the A-CEG Construction Rules set performs in comparison to other A-CEG construction methods. This chapter presents a small-scale controlled experiment where the A-CEG Construction Rules set is compared to the general A-CEG construction guidelines used in industry. The results are promising since the study shows that the A-CEG Construction Rules set is significantly better than the general A-CEG construction guidelines in terms of both effectiveness and efficiency in finding the A-CEG elements in SRSs.

Be aware that there are several limitations to this experiment. First of all, this experiment is clearly based on a small sample size and therefore, one has to take into account the possibility of response bias. A larger-scale experiment is needed to validate our claims. Secondly, the experiment has to be replicated in different contexts. The replications should address changes in the SRSs, for example, using other different application types. The experiment should also be investigated in an industrial setting in order to evaluate whether it still provides positive effects. It would be especially interesting to investigate the method with professionals as subjects. Other further work also includes enhancement of the A-CEG Construction Rules set, either to include checklist items or to develop automation tools to facilitate the identification of A-CEG elements.

Chapter 9: Conclusion and Suggestions for Future Research

9.1 Principal Results of this Study and its Significance

In the software development life cycle, requirements analysis is one of the important phases as any fault in this phase will be carried through the rest of the development. In particular, the SRS, a product of the requirement analysis phase, is so crucial to the success of a software project that it is hard to improve the quality and/or productivity of the project without first addressing the quality of the SRS. Studies revealed that faults made in the requirements phase are extremely expensive to repair and requirements faults are the largest class of faults typically found in a complex software project. Requirements must be correct if the rest of the development effort is to succeed. In order to improve quality and reliability of software continuously throughout the software development life cycle, it is imperative to develop measurement criteria along the life cycle, especially in the early stages. Activities like CEGA which can be carried out in the early phases of software development can ensure software quality and reliability. A review of the literature reveals the scarcity of any publicly reported software measurements related to the detection of problematic requirements and to software reliability prediction at the early stages of software development.

This study focuses on developing an approach to enable the detection of requirements faults and prediction of software reliability at the requirements analysis stage when limited information about the software project is available. The proposed approach is based on the enhanced CEGA, and can be employed for SRS faults detection and reliability prediction in an early stage and possibly throughout the development life cycle. It is shown how the faults in the requirements specifications document can be systematically detected and how the output from the SRS faults detection process can be used as an input to enable the prediction of software reliability in the requirements analysis phase and other development phases. It is demonstrated that the use of the enhanced CEGA as a software reliability measurement tool can be more rigorous and intuitive. Related techniques, methods, and rules are developed to enhance the rigidity, repeatability, and scalability of the approach. The feasibility, usability, and scalability of the approach are experimentally validated.

More specifically, this study accomplishes the following:

- Thoroughly analyzed the advantages, disadvantages, and other technical barriers for CEGA to serve as a software reliability measurement.

- Mathematically formalized CEGA and enhanced its rigidity, repeatability, and scalability toward a solid software reliability measurement. These formal definitions are necessary to ensure that the CEG is meaningful, true and of known accuracy, easy to be stored, represented, and implemented by computers, and can be updated easily in response to the frequent requests for requirements change in practice.

- Developed a CEGA-based taxonomy for SRS faults. One cannot expect to identify types of SRS faults that he or she never ever has thought about or come across. The contribution of the taxonomy lies in providing a systematic way to

205

explore this implicitly existing knowledge by using the heuristics and in increasing the requirements engineer's awareness of the problematic areas in an SRS.

- Developed a two-phase CEGA-based method for SRS faults detection. This method allows software project stakeholders to identify problematic areas in the requirements at a very early development stage. Moreover, this method overcomes the shortcomings of other techniques that fail to ensure complete coverage of functional requirements. According to the cost ratio shown in Figure 2-9, applying our method at the requirements analysis phase could save as much as 99% (or even more) on detecting and fixing the SRS faults if the same SRS faults were not found and fixed until the testing phase.

- Developed a CEGA-based algorithm to quantify the impact of detected faults on software reliability. This is the first method of its kind in the literature. Starting from this method, software project stakeholders are allowed to determine at a very early development stage whether or not the project is at high risk of failure while limited information about the software project is available. They can use the predicted reliability to assess the risks of a project, determine whether a trade-off between new functionalities and the possible loss of reliability is cost-effective, mitigate the risks by removing the major contributor(s), or even cancel the project. However, the topic on how to make decisions based on the reliability predicted at the early stages of software development is beyond the scope of this study. Interested readers are referred to the literature related to risk assessment, risk management and/or decision making [113] for further information.

- Examined the feasibility and scalability of the proposed techniques for detecting SRS faults and predicting the reliability at the requirements analysis phase via two case studies.

- Revealed many aspects of the nature of CEG construction, including

  - collected and distilled patterns in CEG construction.

  - identified and analyzed the influencing factors in CEG construction.

  - provided SRS writers with caveats to avoid common problems found in the practice of specifying SRSs. These problems might cause difficulties in identifying A-CEG elements and lead to increased risks of unreliable software products.

  - developed a set of rules to ease the task of CEG construction. According to the results of Experiment D, the mean accuracy of A-CEG constructors who were using the A-CEG Construction Rules is 8% higher than that of those who were using the general A-CEG construction guidelines, the mean recall 10% higher, and the mean efficiency 13% higher.

- Statistically evaluated the usability of the proposed rules.

- Statistically verified the impact of two influencing factors on using these rules.

The proposed approach provides methods for development teams to detect faults in requirements specification and determine the uncertainty of their impact; it supports trade-off decision and evaluation of remedial actions. The approach is still open for improvement, but it can be concluded that so far the results are inspiring for the future. It will enable software project stakeholders to effectively detect requirements faults and assess the quality of requirements early in development, and ultimately lead to improved software reliability if the identified faults are removed in time. Even with some limitations, the intrinsic advantages of our approach make it attractive from a usability perspective. Software project practitioners (including architects, requirements specialists, designers, coders, testers, and managers), regulators, and policy makers involved in the certification of software systems can benefit most from the techniques proposed in this study.

9.2 Advantages

Our approach has the following advantages/characteristics:

- Our approach is applicable at the requirements analysis phase, a very early stage in the software development lifecycle. One obvious benefit of this characteristic is that fault detection and reliability prediction realized earlier in the software development cycle have a dramatic effect on making software development practices better and more efficient. The CEGA technique discussed in this study can identify potential problem areas in SRSs that may lead to problems or faults in the later development phases. Finding these problem areas in the requirements analysis phase decreases the cost and prevents potential ripple effects from SRS, later in the development life cycle. The primary value gained from utilizing our CEGA-based approach is the capability of systematically analyzing and detecting SRS faults and predicting reliability early in the development process. What makes the approach especially attractive is that CEGA appears to be very effective in detecting other requirements fault types. We have empirically evaluated this broader aspect of the CEGA strategy on a simplified personal access control system and a safety-related real-time control system used for nuclear power plants.

- Our approach distinguishes itself from others by its CEGA-based attribute, which is rigid, methodical, systematic, and therefore uniform, highly repeatable, and reliable. Only a graphical technique such as CEGA may be able to capture the implications in an SRS. CEGA can reveal complexity that may have been hidden by the words alone. It exposes incomplete, incorrect, and ambiguous functional requirements in an SRS.

- Our SRS faults detection methods ensure complete coverage of functional requirements. The SRS analyst can be confident that once CEGA is implemented, the functional requirements are to the best of his/her knowledge faultless, and no ambiguous, incomplete, inconsistent, or incorrect functionality will move into production.

- Many aspects of our approach can be automated.

- Our approach requires only functional requirements and the associated operational profile, which is most likely to be available in the early development stages.

- Our approach is applicable to all types of software systems, although this study focuses on mission-critical systems where a reliable final product has top priority.

9.3 Limitations

This study has a few limitations. Practitioners must carefully weigh these against other options on a case-by-case basis. The limitations of this study are:

1. Our approach assumes that the SRSs are written in plain English text, a primary form to state requirements. Our approach may not be applicable for SRSs specified in some formal languages.

2. Our approach is based on CEGA which uses a CEG to provide a concise representation of logical combinations and corresponding actions specified in an SRS. Be aware that not every aspect of a software system will be specifiable by a CEG. The CEG can only capture functional requirements specified in the SRS and is primarily concerned with modeling inputs and outputs involved in the system to be specified.

3. CEGA will not be able to detect hidden requirements

4. It is unclear how accurate the reliability prediction given by our approach would be. Further research will help answer this question.

5. Implementing our approach is very costly. The most time-consuming task in our approach is to construct an A-CEG from a given informal specification. Automation is a good way to cut down time and cost in A-CEG construction. And we think that A-CEG construction can be partially automated.

6. In general, a significant amount of human intervention is still needed in our approach. The process of identifying SRS faults requires domain knowledge and understanding of the system under study, as well as inspector's creativity, experience, and even intuition. Without prior knowledge of the system, the faults

found through CEGA may not be correct and the final reliability estimation may not be very meaningful. Unfortunately, automatic SRS faults' detection is very difficult.

It might seem that these restrictions eliminate many potential applications. However, despite external appearances, overheads associated with our approach (even without tool support) are lower than the expected benefits which will be incurred by the project. Especially, the cost of using our approach is small compared to the potential major downstream savings because the project teams avoid unnecessary rework and operational problems.

9.4 Suggestions for Future Research

We encourage further studies on the following topics:

- Further Validation of the usability of the A-CEG Construction Rules. Through a small-scale controlled experiment we have assessed the usability of the rules for CEG generation. This has served as a proof of the feasibility and usability of the rules. Due to the intricacy of A-CEG construction and the scarcity of empirical evidence available, there is also a need to further validate our findings by considering SRSs from different domains and explicitly controlling people-related factors, such as SRS analysis expertise in a particular domain.

- Improvement of the A-CEG Construction Rules. The A-CEG Construction Rules set is an attempt to ease A-CEG construction. It is very helpful to add consistency to the way we construct A-CEGs. However, while it still remains useful for A-

CEG construction and can produce significant cost and time savings in CEGA implementation, the rules set is still open to criticism and improvement.

- Automation of our CEGA-based approach. The automation of our approach might be an interesting direction to pursue. There are several aspects of our approach that can be automated:

  1) Conversion between the mathematical expression and graphical expression for a CEG. Graphical techniques are especially valuable for communicating with people who speak different languages. Though informal, unscalable, and unnecessary in our approach, the graphical expression of a CEG helps project stakeholders to find, illustrate, and analyze the software functional requirements, and ease the communication among different project roles. Therefore, it is desirable to develop a tool that will allow convenient conversion between these two CEG formats.

  2) Tools that facilitate the detection of SRS faults. Our SRS fault detection methods are performed by humans through a time-consuming procedure of reading requirements documents and looking for errors. This is tedious at best, and at worst, prone to errors. Even if a complete and general automation of the entire fault detection process is impossible, the most promising approach to improved fault detection is a systematic manual or partially automated procedure. Our methods in conjunction with a powerful analytical tool will provide a rigorous, consistent and cost effective approach to detect SRS faults.

3) Tools that facilitate A-CEG construction. We notice that manually constructing an A-CEG for a bulky SRS is very time-consuming, even with the help of the A-CEG Construction Rules.

4) Identification of failure-relevant inputs. The unified failure-relevant input determination algorithm (shown in Figure 5-5) is ready for automation. Even if doable, it is challenging to manually determine failure-relevant inputs when the number of causes is more than 15.

- Validation of the accuracy of the reliability prediction given by our approach. Although the feasibility and scalability of our approach have been verified using real applications, it is unclear how accurate the reliability predictions given by our CEGA-based approach would be. It has been pointed out [40] that reliability prediction based on process or product measurements alone may not be sufficiently accurate. These predictions need corroboration. In practice, particularly when high levels of reliability need to be assured, it will be necessary to use several sources of evidence to support reliability claims, for instance, evidence of process quality and evidence from software components and structure. Combining such disparate evidence to aid decision making is itself a difficult task. Research in this area is still in a rather early stage. The explosive complexity of today's software systems has made this task even more challenging. Nevertheless we believe this kind of approaches offers the best prospects for accurate reliability prediction and more potential refinement in the future.

213

- Expansion of our approach to other software development phases. A natural extension of this study is to consider applying similar techniques to later products in the life-cycle, such as designs or even source code, where the potential savings are less. We believe that the key characteristics of our approach should apply to other software development phases.

Appendix A: List of Words that Point to Potential Ambiguities (adapted from [70])

Dangling Else

can	could	is one of	must
shall	should	will	would

Ambiguity of Reference

above	below	it	such
the previous	them	these	this
those			

Ambiguous Adjectives

all	any	appropriate	custom
efficient	every	few	frequent
improved	infrequent	intuitive	invalid
many	most	normal	ordinary
rare	same	seamless	several
similar	some	standard	the complete
the entire	transparent	typical	usual
valid			

Ambiguous Adverbs

accordingly	almost	approximately	by and large
commonly	customarily	efficiently	frequently
generally	hardly	ever	in general
infrequently	Intuitively	just about	more often than not
more or less	mostly	nearly	normally
not quite often	on the odd occasion	ordinarily	rarely
roughly	seamlessly	seldom	similarly
sometime	somewhat	transparently	typically
virtually			

215

Ambiguous Variables

the application	the component	the data	the database
the field	the file	the frame	the information
the message	the module	the page	the rule
the screen	the status	the system	the table
the value	the window		

Ambiguous Verbs

adjust	alter	amend	calculate
change	compare	compute	convert
create	customize	derive	determine
edit	enable	improve	Indicate
manipulate	match	maximize	may
minimize	might	modify	optimize
perform	process	produce	provide
support	update	validate	verify

E.G. versus I.E.

e.g.	i.e.

Implicit Cases

also	although	as well	besides
but	even though	for all other	furthermore
however	in addition to	likewise	moreover
still	notwithstanding	otherwise	on the other hand
though	unless	whereas	yet
as required	as necessary		

Temporal Ambiguity

after	annually	at a given time	at the appropriate time
bimonthly	biweekly	daily	every other month
every other week	fast	in a while	later
monthly	quarterly	quickly	soon
twice a month	twice a year	weekly	yearly

Boundary Ambiguity

up to	among	including

Totally Ambiguous

etc.	(sentences that end with "?")

217

Appendix B: Sample Source Code for Calculating the Occurrence Probability of a BDD's Top Node

```
/*********************************************************************
PROGRAM:      BDD' Top Node Occurrence Probability Calculation
FILE:         CEG_main.cpp
FUNCTION:     Constructing a BDD and calculating the top node's occurrence probability
AUTHOR:       Wende Kong
REVISIONS:    02/21/2005 Second release; 10/1/2004 First release
ENVIRONMENT: Visual C++ version 6.0, Pemtium 4/1.0G ; 256mb RAM, Windows XP


NOTES:
```

This C++ program incorporates a software module complied from Binary Decision Diagrams Library Package Version 2.3 (Copyright © 1996, Jorn Lind-Nielsen, All right reserved). This software tool is applicable for other software applications, too, with minor modification. The following steps are required to compile this source code:

(1) Download the file "buddy19.zip" to your computer from

http://www.ee.pdx.edu/~alanmi/research/softports.htm

(2) Unzip the file into a local directory, which will become the home directory of the Buddy static library

(3) Open "Buddy.dsw" in Microsoft Visual C++ 6.0 (click "File -> Open Workspace...")

(4) Click "Executing command Build -> Rebuild All". Ignore the 15 warnings produced by compiling. Thus the buddy.lib is created.

(5) Create an empty project of type "Console Application"

(6) Add this source code the "file source..."

(7) Add "<your_library_path>\buddy\include" to

Project -> Settings -> C/C++ -> Additional include directories

(8) Add "<your_library_path>\buddy\Debug\buddy.lib" to

Project -> Settings -> Link -> Object/library modules

(9) Compile and link the project. An .exe file is created. Execution of this .exe file will yield the occurrence probability of PACS' A-CEG fails. In this sample source code, we assume that the identified failure-relevant inputs are $\bar{c}_1\bar{c}_2\bar{c}_4\bar{c}_5 \cup \bar{c}_1c_2\bar{c}_4\bar{c}_5 \cup c_1\bar{c}_2\bar{c}_4\bar{c}_5$.

```
**********************************************************************/
```

218

```
#include <iostream.h>
#include "bdd.h"

#define N 14
// N is the number of causes plus 1. An extra storage is needed since the first element
// (the one with index 0) of the array is purposely neglected.

float bddProbCal(bdd & currentBdd);

static float NodeProb[N]={0.97,0.97,0.97,0.99,0.97,0.8,0.8,0.8,0.98,0.5,0.5,0.001,0.99};
//NodeProb array stores the probabilities of all causes.
// Pr(c_1)=0.97, Pr(c_2)=0.97, Pr(c_3)=0.97, Pr(c_4)=0.99, Pr(c_5)=0.97, Pr(c_6)=0.8, Pr(c_7)=0.8,
// Pr(c_8)=0.8, Pr(c_9)=0.98, Pr(c_{10})=0.5, Pr(c_{11})=0.5, Pr(c_{12})=0.001, Pr(c_{13})=0.99.

//The following code is corresponding to the revised recursive algorithm shown in
// Figure 5-17.
float bddProbCal(bdd & currentBdd)
{
    float PL, PH, q;
    // consider "High" branch
    if (bdd_high(currentBdd) = = (bdd) 1)
        PH = 1;
    else if (bdd_high(currentBdd) = = (bdd) 0)
        PH = 0;
    else
        PH = bddProbCal(bdd_high(currentBdd));

    // consider "Low" branch
    if (bdd_low(currentBdd) = = (bdd)0)
        PL = 0;
    else if (bdd_low(currentBdd) = = (bdd)1)
        PL = 1;
    else
```

219

```
        PL = bddProbCal(bdd_low(currentBdd));
    q = NodeProb[bdd_var(currentBdd)-1];

    //calculate and return probability value of node
    return (q*PH+(1-q)*PL);
}

void main(void)
{
    int i, j, k;
    bdd c[N+1];      // c[i] is corresponding to c_i. c[0] is not used.
    bdd I_1;         // I_1 is the expression of failure relevant inputs $\overline{c}_1\overline{c}_2\overline{c}_4\overline{c}_5$.
    bdd I_2;         // I_2 is the expression of failure relevant input $\overline{c}_1 c_2\overline{c}_4\overline{c}_5$.
    bdd I_3;         // I_3 is the expression of failure relevant input $c_1\overline{c}_2\overline{c}_4\overline{c}_5$.
    bdd I_ALL;       // I_ALL is the expression of the union of all failure relevant inputs.

    // Initialize the BDD storage.
    bdd_init(100,100);
    bdd_setvarnum(N);

    // The variable order in the final ROBDD is: $c_1$, $c_2$, $c_3$, ..., $c_N$)
    for (i = 1; i <= N; i++)
        c[i] = bdd_ithvar(i);

    I_1 = bdd_not(c[1]) & bdd_not(c[2]) & bdd_not(c[4]) & bdd_not(c[5]);

    I_2 = bdd_not(c[1]) & c[2] & bdd_not(c[4]) & bdd_not(c[5]);

    I_3 = c[1] & bdd_not(c[2]) & bdd_not(c[4]) & bdd_not(c[5]);

    I_ALL= I_1 | I_2 | I_3;
```

```
    cout << "Final Prob=" << bddProbCal(I_ALL) << endl;
}
```

B1. PACS's A-CEG for PACS

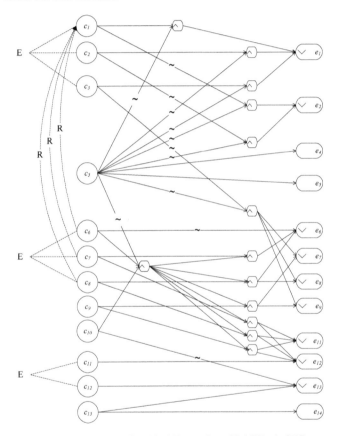

Figure Appendix C-1: Graphical Expression of PACS's A-CEG

$$\hat{C}^A_{PACS} \stackrel{\text{def}}{=} \{c_1;\ c_2;c_3;c_5;c_6;c_7;c_8;c_9;c_{10};c_{11};c_{12;}c_{13}\}$$

$$\hat{E}^A_{PACS} \stackrel{\text{def}}{=} \{e_1;\ e_2;e_4;e_5;e_6;e_7;\ e_8;e_9;e_{11};e_{12};e_{13};e_{14}\}$$

$$\hat{F}^A_{PACS} \stackrel{\text{def}}{=} \left\{ \begin{array}{c}
e_1 := (c_1 \cup c_2 \cup c_3) \cap \bar{c}_5; \\
e_2 := (\bar{c}_1 \cup \bar{c}_2) \cap \bar{c}_5; \\
e_4 := c_5; \\
e_5 := c_5; \\
e_6 := \bar{c}_6 \cup [\bar{c}_5 \cap c_6 \cap c_{10}(c_7 \cup c_8)]; \\
e_7 := \bar{c}_5 \cap [\bar{c}_3 \cup (\cap c_6 \cap c_9 \cap c_{10})]; \\
e_8 := \bar{c}_5 \cap [\bar{c}_3 \cup (\cap c_6 \cap c_8 \cap c_{10})]; \\
e_9 := \bar{c}_5 \cap [\bar{c}_3 \cup (\cap c_6 \cap c_9 \cap c_{10})]; \\
e_{11} := \bar{c}_5 \cap c_6 \cap c_{10} \cap (c_7 \cup c_8 \cup c_9); \\
e_{12} := [\bar{c}_5 \cap c_6 \cap c_{10} \cap (c_7 \cup c_8 \cup c_9)] \cup c_{11}; \\
e_{13} := \bar{c}_{10} \cup c_{12} \cup c_{13}; \\
e_{14} := c_{13}
\end{array} \right\}$$

$$\overline{CON}^A_{PACS} \stackrel{\text{def}}{=} \left\{ \begin{array}{l}
REQUIRE(c_6, c_1); \\
REQUIRE(c_7, c_1); \\
REQUIRE(c_8, c_1); \\
EXCLUSIVE(c_1, c_2, c_3); \\
EXCLUSIVE(c_6, c_7, c_8); \\
EXCLUSIVE(c_{11}, c_{12})
\end{array} \right\}$$

Figure Appendix C-2: Mathematical Expression of PACS's A-CEG

B2.   Identified Faults in PACS' A-CEG

No faults were identified from constructing PACS' A-CEG and conducting ambiguities review. The following faults were detected using the CEG validation algorithm described in Section 4.5.3.

- Wrong Boolean function for effect e_1 (missing cause c_4)

- Wrong Boolean function for effect e_2 (missing cause c_4);

- Missing effect e_3;

- Missing effect e_{10};

B3. PACS' B-CEG

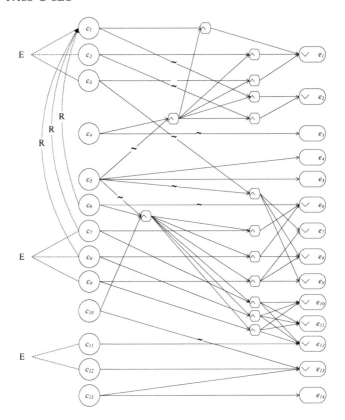

Figure Appendix C-3: Graphical Expression of PACS's B-CEG

$$\hat{C}_{PACS}^B \overset{\text{def}}{=} \{c_1;\ c_2;c_3;c_4;c_5;c_6;c_7;c_8;c_9;c_{10};c_{11};c_{12};c_{13}\}$$

$$\hat{E}_{PACS}^B \overset{\text{def}}{=} \{e_1;\ e_2;e_3;e_4;e_5;e_6;e_7;\ e_8;e_9;e_{10};e_{11};e_{12};e_{13};e_{14}\}$$

$$\hat{F}_{PACS}^B \overset{\text{def}}{=} \left\{ \begin{array}{c} e_1 := (c_1 \cup c_2 \cup c_3) \cap c_4 \cap \bar{c}_5; \\ e_2 := (\bar{c}_1 \cup \bar{c}_2) \cap c_4 \cap \bar{c}_5; \\ e_3 := \bar{c}_4; \\ e_4 := c_5; \\ e_5 := c_5; \\ e_6 := \bar{c}_6 \cup [\bar{c}_5 \cap c_6 \cap c_{10}(c_7 \cup c_8)]; \\ e_7 := \bar{c}_5 \cap [\bar{c}_3 \cup (\cap c_6 \cap c_9 \cap c_{10})]; \\ e_8 := \bar{c}_5 \cap [\bar{c}_3 \cup (\cap c_6 \cap c_8 \cap c_{10})]; \\ e_9 := \bar{c}_5 \cap [\bar{c}_3 \cup (\cap c_6 \cap c_9 \cap c_{10})]; \\ e_{10} := \bar{c}_5 \cap c_6 \cap c_{10} \cap (c_7 \cup c_8 \cup c_9); \\ e_{11} := \bar{c}_5 \cap c_6 \cap c_{10} \cap (c_7 \cup c_8 \cup c_9); \\ e_{12} := [\bar{c}_5 \cap c_6 \cap c_{10} \cap (c_7 \cup c_8 \cup c_9)] \cup c_{11}; \\ e_{13} := \bar{c}_{10} \cup c_{12} \cup c_{13}; \\ e_{14} := c_{13} \end{array} \right\}$$

$$\widehat{CON}_{PACS}^B \overset{\text{def}}{=} \left\{ \begin{array}{c} REQUIRE(c_6, c_1); \\ REQUIRE(c_7, c_1); \\ REQUIRE(c_8, c_1); \\ EXCLUSIVE(c_1, c_2, c_3); \\ EXCLUSIVE(c_6, c_7, c_8); \\ EXCLUSIVE(c_{11}, c_{12}) \end{array} \right\}$$

Figure Appendix C-4: Mathematical Expression of PACS's B-CEG

B4. Definitions of Effects' in PACS' A-CEG and B-CEG

Table Appendix C-1: Definitions of Effects' in PACS' A-CEG and B-CEG

Effect	Description
e_1	Displaying "Enter PIN" on the screen;
e_2	Displaying "Retry" on the screen;
e_3	Displaying "Access Denied" to officer;
e_4	Displaying "Access Denied" on the screen;
e_5	Displaying "System Failure" to officer;
e_6	Displaying "Invalid PIN" on the screen;
e_7	Recording a failed entry into a file;
e_8	Displaying "see officer" to officer;
e_9	Displaying "see officer" on the screen;
e_{10}	Displaying "Please Proceed" on the screen;
e_{11}	Recording and reporting a successful entry;
e_{12}	Opening the gate;
e_{13}	Resetting system and displaying "Insert Card";
e_{14}	Locking the gate.

B5. Identified Failure-relevant Inputs

The identified failure-relevant inputs for PACS are

$$\bar{c}_1\bar{c}_2 c_3\bar{c}_4\bar{c}_{12} \cup \bar{c}_1 c_2\bar{c}_3\bar{c}_4\bar{c}_{12} \cup c_1\bar{c}_2\bar{c}_3\bar{c}_4\bar{c}_{12} \cup \bar{c}_1\bar{c}_2\bar{c}_4\bar{c}_{12} \cup \bar{c}_1 c_2\bar{c}_4\bar{c}_{12} \cup$$

$$c_1\bar{c}_2\bar{c}_4\bar{c}_{12} \cup \bar{c}_4 \cup \bar{c}_4 c_5\bar{c}_6\bar{c}_7 c_9\bar{c}_{12} \cup \bar{c}_4 c_5\bar{c}_6 c_7 c_9\bar{c}_{12} \cup \bar{c}_4 c_5 c_6\bar{c}_7 c_9\bar{c}_{12} \cup$$

$$\bar{c}_3\bar{c}_4\bar{c}_5\bar{c}_8 c_9\bar{c}_{12} \cup \bar{c}_3\bar{c}_4\bar{c}_5\bar{c}_8 c_9\bar{c}_{12} \cup \bar{c}_3\bar{c}_4\bar{c}_5 c_8\bar{c}_9\bar{c}_{12} \cup \bar{c}_3\bar{c}_4\bar{c}_5 c_8 c_9\bar{c}_{12} \cup$$

$$\bar{c}_3 c_4 c_5\bar{c}_8 c_9\bar{c}_{12} \cup \bar{c}_3 c_4 c_5\bar{c}_8 c_9\bar{c}_{12} \cup \bar{c}_3 c_4 c_5 c_8\bar{c}_9\bar{c}_{12} \cup \bar{c}_3 c_4 c_5 c_8 c_9\bar{c}_{12} \cup$$

$$c_3\bar{c}_4 c_5\bar{c}_8 c_9\bar{c}_{12} \cup c_4 c_5\bar{c}_6\bar{c}_7 c_8 c_9\bar{c}_{12} \cup c_4 c_5\bar{c}_6 c_7\bar{c}_8 c_9\bar{c}_{12} \cup c_4 c_5 c_6\bar{c}_7\bar{c}_8 c_9\bar{c}_{12} \cup$$

$$\bar{c}_4 c_5\bar{c}_6\bar{c}_7 c_8 c_9\bar{c}_{12} \cup \bar{c}_4 c_5\bar{c}_6 c_7\bar{c}_8 c_9\bar{c}_{12} \cup \bar{c}_4 c_5 c_6\bar{c}_7\bar{c}_8 c_9\bar{c}_{12} \cup$$

$$\bar{c}_4 c_5\bar{c}_6\bar{c}_7 c_8 c_9\bar{c}_{10}\bar{c}_{12} \cup \bar{c}_4 c_5\bar{c}_6 c_7\bar{c}_8 c_9\bar{c}_{10}\bar{c}_{12} \cup \bar{c}_4 c_5 c_6\bar{c}_7\bar{c}_8 c_9\bar{c}_{10}\bar{c}_{12}$$

B6. PACS' Operation Profile(obtained from [5])

Table Appendix C-2: PACS' OP

Cause	Description	Probability
c_1	Entering a valid card at the first attempt;	0.97
c_2	Entering a valid card at the second attempt;	0.97
c_3	Entering a valid card at the third attempt;	0.97
c_4	Database is available for access;	0.99
c_5	Hardware Failure;	0.001
c_6	Entry of digits of PIN within the 5-seconds time limit;	0.97
c_7	Entering a valid PIN at the first attempt;	0.80
c_8	Entering a valid PIN at the second attempt;	0.80
c_9	Entering a valid PIN at the third attempt;	0.80
c_{10}	Entry of the 1st digit within the 10-seconds time limit;	0.98
c_{11}	Guard Overriding: the guard allows the user to entry;	0.50
c_{12}	Officer resets the system;	0.50
c_{13}	User able to pass within the 30-second time limit after the gate is opened.	0.99

B7. The Predicted Reliability for PACS

Implementing source code similar to Appendix B yields 0.003856, which is corresponding to the occurrence probability of PACS' A-CEG fails. Therefore, the predicted reliability of PACS' is $1 - 0.003856 = 0.996144$.

Appendix D: Descriptions of the Database's Rules in Empirical Study C

Index of Database's Rules	Description
1	An action word related to the application domain should signify an event.
2	Descriptions of actions should signify event(s).
3	• A sentence containing an "if" (followed by Description A) and a "then" (followed by Description B) signifies an IDENTITY relationship between Description A and Description B, when Description A contains none of "or", "and", "not". • Event(s) should be detected for Description A and Description B.
4	• A sentence containing an "if" (followed by Description A1 "and" Description A2) and a "then" (followed by Description B) signifies an AND relationship between Description A1, A2 and Description B, when Description A contains "and". • Event(s) should be detected for Description A1, A2 and Description B.
5	The words "should", "shall", and "must" should signify event(s).
6	If the descriptions of an event contain "and" (e.g. sub-action 1and sub-action2), this event should be represented by the sub-actions.
7	• A sentence containing an "if" (followed by Description A1 "or" Description A2) and a "then" (followed by Description B) signifies an OR relationship between Description A1, A2 and Description B, when Description A contains "and". • Event(s) should be detected for Description A and Description B.
8	If an event is performed by external entities, this event should be a cause.
9	• A sentence containing an "if" (followed by Description A) and a "then" (followed by Description B) signifies a NOT relationship between Description A and Description B, when Description A contains "not". • Event(s) should be detected for Description A and Description B.
10	Actions related to the domain of the application under study should signify events.
11	If an event can be represented by lower-level event(s) that contain more details, use the lower-level event(s) to represent this event.
12	A verb should be regarded as an action word.
13	• A sentence containing an "if" (followed by Description A) and containing an "else" (followed by Description B) signifies a NOT relationship between Description A and Description B. • Event(s) should be detected for Description A and Description B.
14	If the descriptions of an event contain "or", this event should be decomposed into several sub-events.
15	The existence of one of indicators "if", "then" and "else" signifies the existence of the others.
16	All duplicate causes should be removed and represented by only a unique cause.
17	Descriptions on the status of external entities using "is" or "are" should signify a cause(s)
18	If the actor of an event is not specified, this event should be an effect.
19	If events must occur in a time sequence, REQUIRE constraint should be applied to these events sequence.
20	"if" (followed by Description A), "then" (followed by Description B), and "else" (followed by Description C), should be always used together. Omission of any part of Description A, B, and C should be an SRS fault.
21	An event represented by lower-level events should be regarded as duplicate.
22	Any distinct input condition or equivalence class of input conditions should be considered causes.
23	An event in a CEG should be non-decomposable.
24	The Boolean logic of any effect should be expressed in terms of causes.
25	If an event is performed by the application under study, this event should be an effect.

Index of Database's Rules	Description
26	The keywords like "not", "or", "and" etc. signifies logical relationships.
27	Any complicated logical relationships (e.g., XOR, NAND, NOR) should be expressed in terms of four basic logical relationships: IDENTITY, AND, OR, NOT.
28	To avoid duplicate events, only events specified in the functional requirements sections should be included in the CEG.
29	A verb phrase describing action(s) should signify event(s).
30	Events occurring in a time sequence should share same logical relationship.
31	Any inconsistence, incompleteness, incorrectness, ambiguity should be an SRS fault.
32	If the subject of an event is software-related and the subject is not part of the application under study, this event should be a cause.
33	If two or more events occur simultaneously, at least one of the "EXCLUSIVE", "INCLUSIVE" or "ONE-AND-ONLY-ONE" constraints should not be applied to them.
34	A sentence containing an "if" should contain/be followed by description(s) for the "else" option. Omission of description(s) for the "else" option should be an SRS fault.
35	The subject words "application", "algorithm", "system" should signify events.
36	An event must be a non-divisible activity.
37	All duplicate effects should be removed and represented by only a unique effect.
38	If an event is identified as an effect and cannot find any causes, there must be an SRS fault.
39	An "and" between two action words should indicate two events.
40	If an event is performed by human being (e.g., the user), this event should be a cause.
41	None of the descriptive specifications should be considered in identifying effects.
42	Events occurring in a time sequence should be effects if the actor of these events is not specified.
43	If a cause is not linked to any effects, there must be an SRS fault.
44	If an event can be decomposed into several sub-events, this event should be removed from the CEG and represented by the sub-events.
45	Descriptions on the conditions of external entities using "is" or "are" should signify a cause(s)
46	None of the descriptive specifications should be considered in identifying causes.
47	Any TBD (To Be Determined) item related to functional requirements should signify SRS faults. Logical relationships, causes, or effects should not be implied from any SRS faults related to TBD.
48	If the subject of an event is hardware-related (such as RAM, keyboard, In/Out ports, etc.), this event should be a cause.
49	Any implied causes, effects, or logical relationships should be confirmed by a domain expert.
50	For a nesting "if" in forms of If Description 1-1, then Description 1-2; else if Description 2-1, then Description 2-2, else if Description 3-1, then Description 3-2…, the "EXCLUSIVE" constraint should be applied to all events in Description 1-1, 2-1, 3-1, …..
51	All events in the CEG should be unique.
52	When determining the logical relationships, sentence-level rules should have higher precedence than word-level rules.

Appendix E: Reporting Tables Used in Experiment D

Table Appendix E-1: Identified Causes and Effects (for Group I and II)

Sentence No.	Cause/Effect Index	Description
1	e.g.: c_1	e.g.: The user provides the speed value from the keyboard
⋮	⋮	⋮

Table Appendix E-2: Identified Constraints (for Group I and II)

No.	Constraint
1	e.g.: REQUIRE(c_1, c_2)
⋮	⋮

Table Appendix E-3: Identified Logical Relationships (for Group I and II)

No.	Logical Relationship
1	e.g.: $e_1 := c_1 \cup c_2$
⋮	⋮

Table Appendix E-4: Activity-Effort Log Sheet (for Group I and II)

Section No.	Start time	End time	Activities	Percentage, %
1	e.g.: 3:20pm	e.g.: 4:30pm	e.g.: identifying events	e.g.: 10%
			e.g.: removing duplicate events	e.g.: 20%
			…	…
⋮	⋮	⋮	⋮	⋮

Instructions for using Table Appendix E-4:
This table is designed to keep track of your learning process. You will be graded partly on this document. Please follow the instructions carefully.
1. *Record data for each session. A session is any time you start working on the application till you take a break.*
2. *Note the session start time and session end time. A session may be as small as five minutes.*
3. *An activity is anything you do during a session. It can be anything from learning how to use the rules, reading and understanding the specification, applying rules to identify cause, effects, logical relationships, constraints, applying rules to refine the results, to drawing the cause-effect graphs.* ***Record every activity in a Session.***
4. *Be honest and attentive. Although a detailed recording of activities will be appreciated, you need not be creative with your data.*

Table Appendix E-5: Training Activity-Effort Log Sheet (for Group II only)

Section No.	Start time	End time	Training Activities	Duration, in minutes
1			Step 1: Explaining rules	
2			Step 1: Showing an example of applying rules to a sentence	
			Step 2: Practice 1 on applying rules to sentences	
			Step 3: Practice 2 on applying rules to sentences	
3			Step 1: Explaining workflow	
			Step 2: Showing how to use the workflow	
			Step 3: Practice 1 on how to use the workflow	
			Step 4: Practice 2 on how to use the workflow	

231

Table Appendix E-6: Rules to Identify Constraints (for Group II only)

Constraints	Applicable Rules (mark "N/A" if no rules are applicable)
e.g.: REQUIRE(c_1, c_2)	e.g.: Rule 7.9
⋮	⋮

Table Appendix E-7: Rules to Identify to Identify Causes and Effects (for Group II only)

Event index	Cause/Effect	Applicable Rules
e.g.: c_1	e.g.: Cause	e.g. Rule 7.10
⋮	⋮	⋮

Table Appendix E-8: Rules to Identify Logical Relationships (for Group II only)

Logical Relationships	Applicable Rules (mark "N/A" if no rules are applicable)
e.g.: $e_1 := c_1 \cup c_2$	e.g.: Rule 7.5
⋮	⋮

Appendix F: The First Questionnaire Used in Experiment D

Your Name: _____

1. Have you taken the following classes (*Please darken the appropriate option(s)*)?
   Data structure and algorithms   Computer Systems Architecture
   Object-Oriented Programming   Database Design
   Computer Networks   Information Security
   Operating Systems   Compiling Principle
   Computer Graphics   Software Engineering
   Software Testing   Software Safety
   Ensuring Software Reliability and its Integrity

2. Do you have any other professional experience relevant to software engineering?

3. Why did you take the course and what would you most like to get out of the course?

4. What research are you working on?

5. What is recursion? (*Please darken the correct option*)
   A function issues a call to itself
   A function is repetitively called in an application
   An array with infinite number of elements
   Other (Please Specify): _____

6. (a) Which is the fastest sorting algorithm? (*Please darken the correct option*)
   Quick sort   Insertion sort   Bubble sort   Heap sort   Merge sort
   Selection sort   Shell sort   Bin sort (bucket sort)
   Other (Please Specify): _____

   (b) Order these sorting algorithms.

7. What is a function point? (*Please darken the correct option*)
   o It is the main objective of a function as specified in the software requirements specification
   o It is the metric that represents a function's contribution in LOC to the net SLOC. It is expressed as a fraction of the net SLOC.
   o It is a measure of the size of computer applications and the projects that build them. The size is measured from a functional, or user, point of view.
   o None of the above.

8. What is Cause-Effect Graphing technique? (*Please darken the correct option*)
   o It is a black-box testing technique that was originally proposed to generate test cases by transforming a natural language SRS into an acyclic Boolean logic network

o It is a software reliability measurement that aids in identifying requirements that are incomplete and ambiguous.

o It is a computer graphic technique used to render photographic-quality, realistic images

o None of the above

9. Which of the following computer languages have you had experience with? What is your level of expertise?

I have NOT used any of these ever.

I have used the following:

Language	Experience(months)	Expertise Scale (1 -10) (10 is for the strongest level)
C		
C++		
VB		
Java		
SQL		
JSP		
ASP		
HTML		
PHP		
Perl		
other:		

10. Please darken testing techniques that you have ever learned/used.

o Data Flow Testing
o Control Flow Testing
o Loop Testing
o Domain Testing
o Boundary Testing.
o Transaction Flow Testing
o Code Walk-through
o Code Inspection
o Compatibility Testing
o Configuration Testing
o Localization Testing
o Stress Testing
o Performance Testing
o Verification & Validation
o Peer review
o Decision table testing (Cause-effect graphing testing)

Appendix G: Postmortem Questionnaire Used in Experiment D (to assess usability of the A-CEG Construction Rules set)

Your Name: _____

(Please tick the blank most closely corresponding to your feelings on the statements below)

Q. 1: "The CEG technique is useful for me to understand the SRS" (Usefulness)

Strongly Agree   Agree   Neither Agree nor Disagree   Disagree   Strongly Disagree

Q 2: "The CEG technique is very easy, and simple to use" (Ease of Use)

Strongly Agree   Agree   Neither Agree nor Disagree   Disagree   Strongly Disagree

Q 3: "I learned to use the CEG technique quickly" (Ease of Learning)

Strongly Agree   Agree   Neither Agree nor Disagree   Disagree   Strongly Disagree

Q 4: "I am satisfied with the CEG technique" (Satisfaction)

Very good   Good   Fair   Bad   Terrible

Q 5: What is your general impression of the CEG technique? (In general)

Very good   Good   Fair   Bad   Terrible

(Please describe your answers to the below questions)

Q 6: What are the strengths and weaknesses of the CEG technique that you were assigned.

Q 7: What in particular do you like or dislike about the CEG technique? Do you have other comments or suggestions that can help us improve the CEG techniques?

Q 8: In your opinion, under what circumstances and to what extent the assigned technique has the advantages as an A-CEG construction technique, and under what circumstances and to what extent the technique has the disadvantages, why?

Q 9: What are the problems that you found when using the technique?

Glossary

A-CEG	Actually-implemented Cause-Effect Graph
B-CEG	Benchmark Cause-Effect Graph
BDD	Binary Decision Diagram
CEG	Cause-Effect Graph
CEGA	Cause-Effect Graphing Analysis
CMM	Capability Maturity Model
CMMI	Capability Maturity Model Integration
DD	Defect Density measurement
DoD	Department of Defense
FDN	Fault-Days Number measurement
FN	False Negative
FP	False Positive
MIS	Management Information System
O-CEG	Oracle Cause-Effect Graph
PACS	Personal Access Control System
ROBDD	Reduced Ordered Binary Decision Diagram
RSCR	Requirements Specifications Change Request measurement
RT	Requirements Traceability measurement
SRS	Software Requirements Specifications
TN	True Negative
TP	True Positive
UML	Unified Modeling Language
V&V	Verification & Validation

236

Bibliography

[1] IEEE Computer Society, *IEEE standard glossary of software engineering terminology*, 1990. IEEE Std. 610.12-1990.

[2] IEEE Computer Society, *IEEE Standard for a Software Quality Metrics Methodology*, 1998. IEEE Std. 1061-1998.

[3] Lyu, M. R., *Handbook of Software Reliability Engineering*, New York : McGraw-Hill publishing, 1995. ISBN: 0-07-039400-8.

[4] Musa, J. and Okumoto, K., *Software Reliability: Measurement, Prediction, Application*, New York : McGraw-Hill Book Company, 1987. ISBN: 0-07-044093-X.

[5] Li, M., *On the Nature of Relationships Between Measures and Reliability*, Ph.D. Dissertation in Materials and Nuclear Engineering, College Park: University of Maryland, 2002.

[6] Neumann, P. G., *Illustrative Risks to the Public in the Use of Computer Systems and Related Technology*, Feb. 2008,

[7] Li, M. and Smidts, C. S., "A Ranking of Software Engineering Measures Based on Expert Opinion," *IEEE Transactions on Software Engineering*, vol. 29, pp. 811-24, 2003.

[8] Vliet, H. V., *Software Engineering : Principles and Practice*, 3rd Edition, Hoboken, NJ : John Wiley & Sons, 2008. ISBN: 9780470031469.

[9] Chrissis, M. B., Konrad, M. and Shrum, S., *CMMI: Guidelines for Process Integration and Product Improvement*, 2nd Edition, New York : Addison-Wesley Professional, 2006. ISBN-10: 0321279670.

[10] Fenton, N. and Pfleeger, S., *Software Metrics - A Rigorous and Practical Approach*, s.l. : Brooks Cole Publishing Company, 1998. ISBN: 0534954251.

[11] IEEE Computer Society, *IEEE Standard Dictionary of Measures of the Software Aspects of Dependability*, 2006. IEEE Std. 982.1-2005.

[12] Smidts, C. S. and Li, M., *Software Engineering Measures for Predicting Software Reliability in Safety Critical Digital Systems*, Nuclear Regulatory Commission, Office of Nuclear Regulatory Research, Washington DC : USNRC, 2000. Technical Report NUREG/GR-0019.

[13] Boehm, B. W., *Software Cost Estimation with COCOMO II*, Englewood Cliffs : Prentice-Hall, Inc., 2000.

[14] Cook, D. A., "Requirements Risks Can Drown Software Projects," *CrossTalk:The Journal of Defense Software Engineering*, no. 2, 2002. http://www.stsc.hill.af.mil/crosstalk/2002/04/leishman.html.

[15] The Standish Group International, Inc., *the Standish Group CHAOS Report*, 1995. Available online at www.standishgroup.com/chaos.html.

[16] Easterbrook, S., et al., "An Experience Report on Requirements Reliability Engineering Using Formal Methods," *IEEE Transactions on Software Engineering*, vol. 24, no. 1, pp. 4-14, Jan. 1998.

[17] Sheldon, F. et al, "Reliability Measurement from Theory to Practice," *IEEE Software*, vol. 9, no. 4, July 1992.

[18] Martin, J., *An Information Systems Manifesto*, 1st Edition, Upper Saddle River, NJ, USA : Prentice Hall PTR, 1986. ISBN:0134647696.

[19] Software Engineering Institute, *Process Maturity Profile of the Software Community*, 2001.

[20] Leffingwell, D. and Widrig, D., *Managing Software Requirements: A Unified Approach*, Reading, MA : Addison Wesley Publishing Co., 2000. ISBN:0201615932.

[21] Graham, D., Finzi, S. and Glib, T., *Software Inspection*, New York : Addison-Wesley, 1993. ISBN-10: 0201631814.

[22] McConnell, S., *Rapid Development: Taming Wild Software Schedules*, Redmond : Microsoft Press, 1996. p. 72, ISBN: 1-55615-900-5.

[23] "Process Improvement and the Corporate Balance Sheet," *IEEE Software*, vol. 10, no. 4, pp. 28-35, July 1993.

[24] Davis, A. M. and Leffingwell, D. A., *Using Requirements Management to Speed Delivery of Higher Quality Applications*, 1995, available at: http://tinf2.vub.ac.be/~dvermeir/courses/software_engineering/696wp.pdf.

[25] Pfleeger, S. L. and Atlee, J., *Software Engineering: Theory & Practice*, Third Edition, Upper Saddle River : Pearson Education, Inc., 2006. ISBN: 0-13-146913-4.

[26] Kong, W., Shi, Y. and Smidts, C. S., "Early Software Reliability Prediction Using Cause-effect Graphing Analysis," *The 53rd Annual Reliability and Maintainability Symposium (RAMS 2007)*, pp. 173 - 178, January 22-25, 2007.

[27] Lubashevsky, A., "Early Estimation of Software Reliability in Large Telecom Systems," *CrossTalk*, June 2002.

[28] Fagan, M., "Advances in Software Inspections," *IEEE Transactions on Software Engineering*, vol. 12, no. 7, pp. 744-751, July 1986.

[29] Gaffney, J. E. and Davis, C. F., "An Automated Model for Software Early Error Prediction (SWEEP)," *Proceedings of the 13th Minnowbrook Workshop on Software Reliability*, July 1990.

[30] Agreti, W. W. and Evanco, W. M., "Projecting Software Defects from Analyzing Ada Design," *IEEE Transactions on Software Engineering*, vol. 18, no. 11, pp. 988-997, Nov. 1992.

[31] Rome Laboratory, *Methodology for Software Reliability Prediction and Assessment*, 1992. TechRep RL-TR-92-52, Vol. 1-2.

[32] Smidts, C. S., Sova, D. and Mandela, G. K., "An Architectural Model for Software Reliability Quantification," *The Eighth International Symposium On Software Reliability Engineering*, vols. 2-5 Nov., pp. 324 - 335, 1997.

[33] Smidts, C. S., Stutzke, M. and Stoddard, R. W., "Software Reliability Modeling: An Approach to Early Reliability Prediction," *IEEE Transactions on Reliability*, vol. 47, no. 3, pp. 268-278, September 1998.

[34] Yin, M.L., Hyde, C. L. and James, L. E., "A Petri-Net Approach for Early-Stage System-Level Software Reliability Estimation," *Proceedings of Annual Reliability and Maintainablity Symposium (RAMS'00)*, pp. 100-105, 2000.

[35] Zhao, J., Liu, H. and Yang, X., "Early Stage Software Reliability Estimation with Stochastic Reward Nets," *Journal of Donghua University(English Edition)*, no. 3, 2003.

[36] Tripathi, R. and Mall, R., "Early Stage Software Reliability and Design Assessment," *12th Asia-Pacific Software Engineering Conference (APSEC'05)*, pp. 619-628, 2005.

[37] Hu, Q. P., et al., "Early Software Reliability Prediction with Extended ANN Model," *Proceedings of the 30th Annual International Computer Software and Applications Conference (COMPSAC'06)*, vol. 02, pp. 234 - 239, 2006.

[38] Mei, D., "Early Software Reliability Prediction with Wavelet Networks Models," *The 2007 International Conference on Intelligent Systems and Knowledge Engineering*, Oct. 15-16, 2007.

[39] Cheung, L., et al., "Early Prediction of Software Component Reliability," *Proceedings of the 30th International Conference on Software Engineering (ICSE' 08)*, pp. 111-120, May 10-18, 2008.

[40] Smidts, C. S., et al., *A Large Scale Validation of a Methodology for Assessing Software Quality*, Office of Nuclear Regulatory Research, Washington, DC : USNRC, 2009 (submitted but not yet published).

[41] Jones, C., *Measuring Global Software Quality*, Burlington, MA : s.n., 1995.

[42] IEEE Computer Society, *IEEE Standard Dictionary of Measures to Produce Reliable Software*, 1988. IEEE Std. 982.1-1988.

[43] Lawrence, J. D., et al., *Assessment of Software Reliability Measurement Methods for Use in Probabilistic Risk Assessment*, Fission Energy and Systems Safety Program, Lawrence Livermore Nationall Laboratory, 1998. Technical Report UCRLID-136035.

[44] Li, M., et al., "Validation of a Methodology for Assessing Software Reliability," *Proceedings of the 15th International Symposium on Software Reliability Engineering (ISSRE'04)*, pp. 66- 76, Nov. 2-5, 2004.

[45] Myers, G. J., et al., *The Art of Software Testing*, 2nd Edition, Hoboken : John Wiley & Sons, Inc., 2004. pp. 65-88, ISBN: 0-471-46912-2.

[46] Elmendorf, W. R., *Cause-effect Graphs in Functional Testing*, Poughkeepsie, NY : IBM Systems Development Division, 1973. TR-00.2487.

[47] *Software Reliability: Principle and Practices*, New York : Wiley-Interscience Inc., 1976. pp. 218-227, ISBN: 0-471-62765-8..

[48] Nursimulu, K. and Probert, R. L., "Cause-Effect Graphing Analysis and Validation of Requirements," *Proceeding of the 1995 Conference of the Centre for Advanced Studies on Collaborative Research*, pp. 46-61, Nov. 1995.

[49] Paradkar, A., "On the Experience of Using Cause-Effect Graphs for Software Specification and Test Generation," *IBM Press*, p. 51, 1994.

[50] Paradkar, A., Tai, K. C. and Vouk, M. A., "Specification-based testing using cause-effect graphs," *Annals of Software Engineering*, vol. 4, pp. 133 - 157, 1997.

[51] Bender RBT Inc., *BenderRBT Cause-Effect Graphing Users Guide*, 2006, retrieved August 2nd, 2008 http://www.benderrbt.com/BenderRBT-Cause-Effect%20Graphing%20User%20Guide.pdf.

[52] Le, J. C., *Perspectives on Software Requirements*, Boston : Kluwer Academic Publishers Group, 2004. ISBN: 1-4020-7625-8.

[53] IEEE Computer Society, *IEEE Recommended Practice for Software Requirements Specifications*, 1998. ANSI/IEEE Standard 830-1998.

[54] Davis, A., *Software Requirements: Objects, Functions, and States*, Englewood Cliff, NJ : Prentice Hall, 1993.

[55] Schneider, G. M., Martin, J. and Tsai, W. T., "An experimental Study of Fault Detection in User Requirements Documents," *ACM Transactions on Software Engineering and Methodddology*, vol. 1, no. 22, pp. 188-204, 1992.

[56] Gause, D. C. and Weinberg, G. M., *Exploring Requirements: Quality Before Design*, New York, NY : Dorset House, 1989.

[57] Kamsties, E., *Surfacing Ambiguity in Natural language Requirements*, Ph.D. Dissertation, Fachbereich Informatik, University Kaiserslautern, Germany, 2001.

[58] Weißleder, S. and Sokenou, D., "Cause-Effect Graphs for Test Models Based on UML and OCL,"

[59] Paradkar, A., Tai, K.C. and Vouk, M., "Automated test generation for cause-effect graphs," *IEEE Transactions on Reliability*, vol. 45, pp. 515-530, 1996.

[60] Boris, B., *Software Testing Techniques*, 2nd Edition, New York : Van Nostrand Reinhold, Inc., 1990.

[61] Ostrand, T. J. and Balcer, M. J., "The category-partition method for specifying and generating fuctional tests," *Communications of the ACM*, vol. 31, no. 6, 1988.

[62] Copeland, L., *A Practitioner's Guide to Software Test Design*, Norwood : Artech House, 2004. ISBN:158053791x.

[63] Ghose, S., *Software Requirements Specifications for LOCAT*, College Park, MD, USA : University of Maryland, 2004.

[64] U.S. National Aeronautics and Space Administration (NASA), *NASA Software Documentation Standard - Software Engineering Program* , July 1991. NASA-STD-2100-91.

[65] U.S. Department of Defense, *Software Development and Documentation*, Philadelphia : Naval Publications and Forms Center, Dec. 1994. MIL-STD-498 Military Standard.

[66] ISO/IEC, *Systems and software engineering - Software life cycle processes*, s.l. : International Organization for Standardization/International Electrotechnical Commission, 2008. ISO/IEC 12207:2008.

[67] Hammer, T. F., Huffman, L. L. and Rosenberg, L. H., "Doing Requirements Right the First Time," *Crosstalk, Journal of Defense Software Engineering*, December 1998.

[68] Hayes, J. H., "Building a Requirement Fault Taxonomy: Experiences from a NASA Verification and Validation Research Project," *Proceedings of the 14th International Symposium on Software Reliability Engineering (ISSRE'03)*, pp. 49- 59, Nov. 2003.

[69] IEEE Computer Society, *IEEE Standard for Software Verification and Validation*, 2004. IEEE Std 1012-2004.

[70] Ryser, J., Berner, S. and Glinz, M., *On the State of the Art in Requirements-based Validation and Test of Software*, Zurich, Switzerland : the University of Zurich, 1998. Available at: ftp://ftp.ifi.unizh.ch/pub/techreports/TR-98/ifi-98.12.pdf.

[71] Rumbaugh, J. and Jacobson, I., *The Unified Modeling Language Reference Manual*, Boston : Addison-Wesley, 1999.

[72] Spivey, J. M., *The Z Notation: A Reference Manual*, 2nd Edition, London : Prentice-Hall, 1992.

[73] Abrial, J. R., *The B Book - Assigning Programs to Meanings*, England : Cambridge University Press, 1996.

[74] Porter, A. A., Votta, L. G. and Basili, V. R., "Comparing Detection Methods For Software Requirements Inspections: A Replicate Experiment," *IEEE Transactions on Software Engineering*, vol. 21, no. 6, pp. 563 - 575, 1995.

[75] Mendenhall, W., Beaver, R. J. and Beaver, B., *Introduction to Probability and Statistics*, 13th Edition, Belmont : Duxbury Press, 2008. p. 159, ISBN-10: 0495389536.

[76] Hoffman, D., "A Taxonomy for Test Oracles," *Quality Week '98*, 1998.

[77] Whitesitt, J. E., *Boolean Algebra and Its Applications*, Mineola, NY, USA : Dover Publications, 1995. 0486684830..

[78] Gregg, J. R., *Ones and Zeros: Understanding Boolean Algebra, Digital Circuits, and the Logic of Sets*, Hoboken : Wiley-IEEE Press, 1998. 978-0780334267..

[79] Bryant, R. E., "Graph Based Algorithms for Boolean," *IEEE Transactions on Computer Engineering*, vols. C-35, no. no. 8, pp. 677-691, Aug. 1986.

[80] Reay, K. A. and Andrews, J. D., "A Fault Tree Analysis Strategy Using Binary Decision Diagrams," *Reliability Engineering and System Safety*, vol. 78, no. 1, pp. 45-56, 2002.

[81] Bryant, R. E., "Graph-Based Algorithms for Boolean Function Manipulation," *IEEE Transactions on Computers*, vol. 35, no. 8, pp. 677-691, August 1986.

[82] IT-University of Copenhagen (ITU), *BuDDy: Binary Decision Diagram papckage Release 2.2*, 2002.

[83] Walton, G. H., Poore, J. H. and Trammell, C. J., "Statistical Testing of Software Based on a Usage Model," *Software Practice & Experience*, vol. 25, no. 11, pp. 97-108, January 1995.

[84] Musa, J., "The operational profile in software reliability engineering: an overview," *Proceedings of 3rd International Symposium on Software Reliability Engineering*, pp. 140-154, Oct. 7-10, 1992.

[85] Sandfoss, R.V. and Meyer, S. A., "Input Requirements needed to Produce an Operational Profile for a New Telecommunications System," *Proceedings of the Eighth International Symposium on Software Reliability Engineering (ISSRE '97)*, pp. 29 - 39, Nov. 2-5, 1997.

[86] Elbaum, S. and Narla, S., "A Methodology for Operational Profile Refinement," *Proceedings of the 2001 Annual Reliability and Maintainability Symposium (RAMS 2001)*, pp. 142 - 149, Jan. 22-25, 2001.

[87] Gittens, M., Lutfiyya, H. and Bauer, M., "An Extended Operational Profile Model," *Proceedings of the 15th International Symposium on Software Reliability (ISSRE 2004)*, pp. 314- 325, Nov. 2-5, 2004.

[88] Lockheed Martin Corporation Inc., *PACS (Personal Access Control System) Requirements Specification*, Gaithersburg, MD : Lockheed Martin Corporation Inc., 1998.

[89] Center for Computer-Integrated Surgical Systems and Technology (CISST), *Software Requirements Specification for MRC-II System*, Baltimore, MD : Johns Hopkins University, 2003.

[90] DPUSRS-01, *Software Requirements Specifications for the Instrument A Data Processing Unit for the Company X Gamma Ray Burst Explorer*, 2003.

[91] Raytheon TI Systems, *Software Requirements Sepcification for the Long Range Advanced Scout Surveillance System (LRAS3),* 1997.

[92] Brossat, JeanPhilippe, *Software Requirements Specification for Qheadache, Version 1.0,* 2003.

[93] Department of Computer Science, University of Toronto, *Software Requirements Specification for the Graph Editor,* 2001.

[94] Amoson, J., et al., *Software Requirements Specification for the "Software Engineering Tool",* 2001.

[95] Acorn Software, *Bus Tracking System Software Requirements Specification,* 2006.

[96] Tayyab, A. A., *Software Requirements Specifications forFloristExchange Project,* 2001.

[97] Fox, J., et al., *Software Requirements Specifications:PICASSO,* s.l. : Computer Science Dept., Univ. Alabama in Huntsville, 1997. Technical Report TR-UAH-CS-1997-04.

[98] Kao, A. and Poteet, S. R., *Natural Language Processing and Text Mining,* New York : Springer Publishing Company, 2006. ISBN-13: 978-1846281754..

[99] Shneiderman, B., *Designing the user interface: Strategies for effective human-computer interaction,* MA : Addison-Wesley, 1987.

[100] Labbe, C. and Labbe, D., "Inter-Textual Distance and Authorship Attribution," *Journal of Quantitative Linguistics,* vol. 8, no. 3, pp. 213-231, 2001.

[101] Labbe, C. and Labbe, D., "A Tool for literary studies- Intertexual Distance and Tree Classification," *Literary and Linguistic Computing,* vol. 21, no. 3, pp. 311-326, 2006.

[102] Peck, R. and Devore, J. L., *Statistics: The Exploration & Analysis of Data,* Pacific Grove, CA : Duxbury Press, 2007. ISBN-13: 978-0495390879.

[103] Jones, C., *Applied Software Measurement: Assuring Productivity and Quality,* 2nd Edition, New York : McGraw-Hill, 1996. ISBN: 0070328269.

[104] Box, G. E., Hunter, J. S. and Hunter, W. G., *Statistics for Experimenters: Design, Innovation, and Discovery,* 2nd Edition, New York : Wiley-Interscience, 2005. ISBN: 0471718130.

[105] Image Processing Group, University of Zagreb, *CHAIRMAN - Conference Management System Software Requirements Specification (SRS),* 2004.

[106] GRUPPE 13, *IMS Software Requirement Specification,* June, 2003.

[107] Ghose, S., *Software Requirements Specification for Student Registry Query System (SRQS),* College Park, MD, USA : University Maryland, 2004.

[108] Ghose, S., *Software Requirements Specifications for SSP,* College Park, MD, USA : University of Maryland, 2004.

[109] Ghose, S., *Software Requirements Specifications for TELLERFAST,* College Park, MD, USA : University of Maryland, 2004.

[110] The Themas Team, *The Energy Management System Software Requirements Specifications,* 1998.

[111] Ghose, S., *Software Requirements Specifications for an Word Processor Unit (WPU),* College Park, MD, USA : University of Maryland, 2004.

[112] Raynald Levesque and SPSS Inc., *Programming and Data Management for SPSS® Statistics 17.0 A Guide for SPSS Statistics and SAS® Users,* Chicago, IL : SPSS Inc., 2008.

[113] Koller, G., *Risk Modeling for Determining Value and Decision Making,* FL: Boca Raton : Chapman & Hall/CRC, 2000. ISBN-13: 978-1584881674.

[114] Hastie, S., Software Quality: The Missing X-Factor, June 2002, http://www.softed.com/Resources/WhitePapers/SoftQual_XFactor.aspx.

[115] Leonard, J. G. and Nordgren, R. K., *An Analysis of Early Software Reliability Improvement Techniques,* 1997. Master's thesis.

[116] Rome Laboratory, "Methodology for Software Reliability Estimation and Assessment," vol. 1 and 2, 1992. Technical Report RLTR- 92-52.

[117] Guvenc, M., "Writing Testable and Code-able Requirements," *BorCon 2004 Proceedings,* September 11-25, 2004.

[118] Smidts, C. S. and Li, M., *Validation of A Methodology for Assessing Software Quality,* Nuclear Regulatory Commission, Office of Nuclear Regulatory Research, Washington DC : USNRC, 2004. NUREG/CR-6848.

[119] Smidts, C. S. and Li, M., *Preliminary Validation of a Methodology for Assessing Software Quality,* University of Maryland, Washington, DC : U.S. Nuclear Regulatory Commission, 2004. NUREG/CR-6848.

[120] Wohlin, C. and Runeson, P., "A Method Proposal for Early Software Reliability Estimations," *Proceedings of 3rd International Symposium on Software Reliability Engineering,* pp. 156-163, 1992.

[121] "An Enhanced Model for Early Software Reliability Prediction Using Software Engineering Metrics," *2008 Second International Conference on Secure System Integration and Reliability Improvement (SSIRI'08),* pp. 177-178, 2008.

[122] Nagappan, N., "Towards a Metric Suite for Early Software Reliability Assessment," *Proceedings of the 26th International Conference on Software Engineering,* pp. 60 - 62, 2004.

[123] Smith, C. and Uber, C., "Experience Report on Early Software Reliability Prediction and Estimation," *Proceedings of the 10th International Symposium on Software Reliability Engineering,* p. 282, 1999.

[124] Shi, Y., Kong, W. and Smidts, C. S., "Data Collection and Analysis for the Reliability Prediction and Estimation of a Safety Critical System," *Reliability Analysis of System Failure Data (RAF'07),* March 1-2, 2007. Available at http://www.deeds.informatik.tu-darmstadt.de/RAF07/papers/wende_kong.pdf.

[125] IEEE Computer Society, *IEEE Recommended Practice for Software Requirements Specifications,* 1993. ANSI/IEEE Standard 830-1993.

[126] Ghose, S., *Software Requirements Specifications for LOCAT-II,* College Park, MD, USA : University of Maryland, 2004.

[127] *Requirements Specification for Personal Access Control System,* Gaithersburg, MD, USA : Lockheed Martin Corporation Inc., 1998.

[128] Gilb, T. and Graham, D., *Software Inspection,* New York : Addison-Wesley, 1994.

[129] Fagan, M. E., "Design and code inspections to reduce errors in program development," *IBM Systems Journal,* vol. 15, no. 3, pp. 182-211, 1976.

[130] Carver, J. C., Nagappan, N. and Page, A., "The Impact of Educational Background on the Effectiveness of Requirements Inspections: An Empirical Study," *IEEE Transactions on Software Engineering,* vol. 34, no. 6, pp. 800-812, Nov/Dec 2008.